MznLnx

Missing Links Exam Preps

Exam Prep for

Essentials of Marketing Research

Hair et al..., 1st Edition

The MznLnx Exam Prep is your link from the texbook and lecture to your exams.
The MznLnx Exam Preps are unauthorized and comprehensive reviews of your textbooks.

MznLnx

Rico
Publications

Exam Prep for Essentials of Marketing Research
1st Edition
Hair et al...

Publisher: Raymond Houge
Assistant Editor: Michael Rouger
Text and Cover Designer: Lisa Buckner
Marketing Manager: Sara Swagger
Project Manager, Editorial Production: Jerry Emerson
Art Director: Vernon Lowerui

Product Manager: Dave Mason
Editorial Assitant: Rachel Guzmanji
Pedagogy: Debra Long
Cover Image: Jim Reed/Getty Images
Text and Cover Printer: City Printing, Inc.
Compositor: Media Mix, Inc.

Printed in the United States
ISBN:

For more information about our products, contact us at:
Dave.Mason@RicoPublications.com

For permission to use material from this text or product, submit a request online to:
Dave.Mason@RicoPublications.com

Contents

TO THE STUDENT

COMPREHENSIVE

The *MznLnx* Exam Prep series is designed to help you pass your exams. Editors at MznLnx review your textbooks and then prepare these practice exams to help you master the textbook material. Unlike study guides, workbooks, and practice tests provided by the texbook publisher and textbook authors, *MznLnx* gives you ***all*** of the material in each chapter in exam form, not just samples, so you can be sure to nail your exam.

MECHANICAL

The MznLnx Exam Prep series creates exams that will help you learn the subject matter as well as test you on your understanding. Each question is designed to help you master the concept. Just working through the exams, you gain an understanding of the subject--its a simple mechanical process that produces success.

INTEGRATED STUDY GUIDE AND REVIEW

MznLnx is not just a set of exams designed to test you, its also a comprehensive review of the subject content. Each exam question is also a review of the concept, making sure that you will get the answer correct without having to go to other sources of material. You learn as you go! Its the easiest way to pass an exam.

HUMOR

Studying can be tedious and dry. MznLnx's instructional design includes moderate humor within the exam questions on occassion, to break the tedium and revitalize the brain

1. A _________ is a collection of symbols, experiences and associations connected with a product, a service, a person or any other artifact or entity.

_________s have become increasingly important components of culture and the economy, now being described as 'cultural accessories and personal philosophies'.

Some people distinguish the psychological aspect of a _________ from the experiential aspect.

a. Store brand
b. Brand equity
c. Brand
d. Brandable software

2. The _________ is a professional association for marketers. As of 2008 it had approximately 40,000 members. There are collegiate chapters on 250 campuses.
a. American Marketing Association
b. ACNielsen
c. ADTECH
d. AMAX

3. _________ consists of the processes a company uses to track and organize its contacts with its current and prospective customers. _________ software is used to support these processes; information about customers and customer interactions can be entered, stored and accessed by employees in different company departments. Typical _________ goals are to improve services provided to customers, and to use customer contact information for targeted marketing.
a. Product bundling
b. Demand generation
c. Commercialization
d. Customer relationship management

4. _________ is defined by the American _________ Association as the activity, set of institutions, and processes for creating, communicating, delivering, and exchanging offerings that have value for customers, clients, partners, and society at large. The term developed from the original meaning which referred literally to going to market, as in shopping, or going to a market to sell goods or services.

_________ practice tends to be seen as a creative industry, which includes advertising, distribution and selling.

a. Marketing myopia
b. Product naming
c. Customer acquisition management
d. Marketing

5. Consumer market research is a form of applied sociology that concentrates on understanding the behaviours, whims and preferences, of consumers in a market-based economy, and aims to understand the effects and comparative success of marketing campaigns. The field of consumer _________ as a statistical science was pioneered by Arthur Nielsen with the founding of the ACNielsen Company in 1923 .

Thus _________ is the systematic and objective identification, collection, analysis, and dissemination of information for the purpose of assisting management in decision making related to the identification and solution of problems and opportunities in marketing.

a. Marketing research
b. Marketing research process
c. Logit analysis
d. Focus group

6. _________ is a form of marketing developed from direct response marketing campaigns conducted in the 1970's and 1980's which emphasizes customer retention and satisfaction, rather than a dominant focus on 'point of sale' transactions.

_________ differs from other forms of marketing in that it recognizes the long term value to the firm of keeping customers, as opposed to direct or 'Intrusion' marketing, which focuses upon acquisition of new clients by targeting majority demographics based upon prospective client lists.

_________ refers to long-term and mutually beneficial arrangement wherein both buyer and seller focus on value enhancement through the certain of more satisfying exchange.This approach attempts to transcend the simple purchase exchange process with customer to make more meaningful and richer contact by providing a more holistic, personalized purchase, and use orn consumption experience to create stronger ties.

a. Global marketing
b. Diversity marketing
c. Relationship marketing
d. Guerrilla Marketing

7. _________ is a set of six steps which defines the tasks to be accomplished in conducting a marketing research study. These include problem definition, developing an approach to problem, research design formulation, field work, data preparation and analysis, and report generation and presentation.

a. Preference-rank translation
b. Marketing research process
c. Market analysis
d. Simple random sampling

8. Customer _________ consists of the processes a company uses to track and organize its contacts with its current and prospective customers. CRelationship management software is used to support these processes; information about customers and customer interactions can be entered, stored and accessed by employees in different company departments. Typical CRelationship management goals are to improve services provided to customers, and to use customer contact information for targeted marketing.
a. Product bundling
b. Marketing
c. Green marketing
d. Relationship management

9. A personal and cultural _________ is a relative ethic _________, an assumption upon which implementation can be extrapolated. A _________ system is a set of consistent _________s and measures that is soo not true. A principle _________ is a foundation upon which other _________s and measures of integrity are based.
a. Perceptual maps
b. Value
c. Supreme Court of the United States
d. Package-on-Package

10. _________ refer to a collection of facts usually collected as the result of experience, observation or experiment or a set of premises. This may consist of numbers, words particularly as measurements or observations of a set of variables. _________ are often viewed as a lowest level of abstraction from which information and knowledge are derived.
a. Data
b. Pearson product-moment correlation coefficient
c. Sample size
d. Mean

11. _________ can be regarded as an outcome of mental processes (cognitive process) leading to the selection of a course of action among several alternatives. Every _________ process produces a final choice. The output can be an action or an opinion of choice.

a. 6-3-5 Brainwriting
b. Decision making
c. 180SearchAssistant
d. Power III

12. _________ in organizations and public policy is both the organizational process of creating and maintaining a plan; and the psychological process of thinking about the activities required to create a desired goal on some scale. As such, it is a fundamental property of intelligent behavior. This thought process is essential to the creation and refinement of a plan, or integration of it with other plans, that is, it combines forecasting of developments with the preparation of scenarios of how to react to them.
a. 180SearchAssistant
b. 6-3-5 Brainwriting
c. Planning
d. Power III

13. Competitiveness is a comparative concept of the ability and performance of a firm, sub-sector or country to sell and supply goods and/or services in a given market. Although widely used in economics and business management, the usefulness of the concept, particularly in the context of national competitiveness, is vigorously disputed by economists, such as Paul Krugman .

The term may also be applied to markets, where it is used to refer to the extent to which the market structure may be regarded as perfectly _________.

a. Competitive
b. Geographical pricing
c. Customs union
d. Free trade zone

14. _________ is a methodology in the social sciences for studying the content of communication. Earl Babbie defines it as 'the study of recorded human communications, such as books, websites, paintings and laws.' It is most commonly used by researchers in the social sciences to analyze recorded transcripts of interviews with participants.

_________ is also considered a scholarly methodology in the humanities by which texts are studied as to authorship, authenticity, of meaning.

a. 6-3-5 Brainwriting
b. Power III
c. 180SearchAssistant
d. Content analysis

15. A _________ is a documented investigation of a Market that is used to inform a firm's planning activities particularly around decision of: inventory, purchase, work force expansion/contraction, facility expansion, purchases of capital equipment, promotional activities, and many other aspects of a company.

Not all managers are asked to conduct a _________, but all managers must make decisions using _________ data and understand how the data was derived. So all managers need a reasonable understanding of the tools most used for making sales forecasts and analyzing markets.

a. Simple random sampling
b. Cross tabulation
c. Preference regression
d. Market analysis

16. A _________ is a subgroup of people or organizations sharing one or more characteristics that cause them to have similar product and/or service needs. A true _________ meets all of the following criteria: it is distinct from other segments (different segments have different needs), it is homogeneous within the segment (exhibits common needs); it responds similarly to a market stimulus, and it can be reached by a market intervention. The term is also used when consumers with identical product and/or service needs are divided up into groups so they can be charged different amounts.
a. Customer insight
b. Commercial planning
c. Production orientation
d. Market segment

17. _________ is a marketing term, and involves evaluating the situation and trends in a particular company's market. _________ is often called the 'three c's', which refers to the three major elements that must be studied:

- Customers
- Costs
- Competition

The number of 'c's' is sometimes extended to four, five, or even six, with 'Collaboration', 'Company', and 'Competitive advantage'.

- Marketing mix
- SWOT analysis

.

a. 180SearchAssistant
b. 6-3-5 Brainwriting
c. Power III
d. Situation analysis

18. A _________ is a form of qualitative research in which a group of people are asked about their attitude towards a product, service, concept, advertisement, idea, or packaging. Questions are asked in an interactive group setting where participants are free to talk with other group members.

Ernest Dichter originated the idea of having a 'group therapy' for products and this process is what became known as a _________.

a. Cross tabulation
b. Marketing research process
c. Logit analysis
d. Focus group

19. _________ was originally coined by Austrian psychologist Alfred Adler in 1929. The current broader sense of the word dates from 1961.

In sociology, a _________ is the way a person lives.

a. Lifestyle
b. 180SearchAssistant
c. 6-3-5 Brainwriting
d. Power III

20. _________ is a graphics technique used by asset marketers that attempts to visually display the perceptions of customers or potential customers. Typically the position of a product, product line, brand, or company is displayed relative to their competition.

Perceptual maps can have any number of dimensions but the most common is two dimensions.

a. Kano model
b. Customer franchise
c. Market environment
d. Perceptual mapping

21. In marketing, _________ has come to mean the process by which marketers try to create an image or identity in the minds of their target market for its product, brand, or organization. It is the 'relative competitive comparison' their product occupies in a given market as perceived by the target market.

Re-_________ involves changing the identity of a product, relative to the identity of competing products, in the collective minds of the target market.

a. Containerization
b. GE matrix
c. Moratorium
d. Positioning

22. A _________, in the field of business and marketing, is a geographic region or demographic group used to gauge the viability of a product or service in the mass market prior to a wide scale roll-out. The criteria used to judge the acceptability of a _________ region or group include:

1. a population that is demographically similar to the proposed target market; and
2. relative isolation from densely populated media markets so that advertising to the test audience can be efficient and economical.

The _________ ideally aims to duplicate 'everything' - promotion and distribution as well as `product' - on a smaller scale. The technique replicates, typically in one area, what is planned to occur in a national launch; and the results are very carefully monitored, so that they can be extrapolated to projected national results. The `area' may be any one of the following:

- Television area
- Test town
- Residential neighborhood
- Test site

A number of decisions have to be taken about any _________:

- Which _________?
- What is to be tested?
- How long a test?
- What are the success criteria?

The simple go or no-go decision, together with the related reduction of risk, is normally the main justification for the expense of _________s. At the same time, however, such _________s can be used to test specific elements of a new product's marketing mix; possibly the version of the product itself, the promotional message and media spend, the distribution channels and the price.

a. Preadolescence
b. 180SearchAssistant
c. Power III
d. Test market

23. In economics, business, retail, and accounting, a _________ is the value of money that has been used up to produce something, and hence is not available for use anymore. In economics, a _________ is an alternative that is given up as a result of a decision. In business, the _________ may be one of acquisition, in which case the amount of money expended to acquire it is counted as _________.

a. Variable cost
b. Fixed costs
c. Transaction cost
d. Cost

24. A _________ is a process that can allow an organization to concentrate its limited resources on the greatest opportunities to increase sales and achieve a sustainable competitive advantage. A _________ should be centered around the key concept that customer satisfaction is the main goal.

A _________ is most effective when it is an integral component of corporate strategy, defining how the organization will successfully engage customers, prospects, and competitors in the market arena.

a. Psychographic
b. Marketing strategy
c. Cyberdoc
d. Societal marketing

25. A _________ is a plan of action designed to achieve a particular goal.

_________ is different from tactics. In military terms, tactics is concerned with the conduct of an engagement while _________ is concerned with how different engagements are linked.

a. 6-3-5 Brainwriting
b. Power III
c. Strategy
d. 180SearchAssistant

26. _________, a business term, is a measure of how products and services supplied by a company meet or surpass customer expectation. It is seen as a key performance indicator within business and is part of the four perspectives of a Balanced Scorecard.

In a competitive marketplace where businesses compete for customers, _________ is seen as a key differentiator and increasingly has become a key element of business strategy.

a. Customer base
b. Supplier diversity
c. Psychological pricing
d. Customer satisfaction

27. _________ is one of the four elements of marketing mix. An organization or set of organizations (go-betweens) involved in the process of making a product or service available for use or consumption by a consumer or business user.

The other three parts of the marketing mix are product, pricing, and promotion.

a. Comparison-Shopping agent
b. Distribution
c. Better Living Through Chemistry
d. Japan Advertising Photographers' Association

28. _________ are used to collect quantitative information about items in a population. Surveys of human populations and institutions are common in political polling and government, health, social science and marketing research. A survey may focus on opinions or factual information depending on its purpose, and many surveys involve administering questions to individuals.

a. Gross Margin Return on Inventory Investment
b. Statistical surveys
c. BeyondROI
d. Convergent

29. _________ is a term used by project managers and project management (PM) organizations to describe methods for analyzing and collectively managing a group of current or proposed projects based on numerous key characteristics. The fundamental objective of the _________ process is to determine the optimal mix and sequencing of proposed projects to best achieve the organization's overall goals - typically expressed in terms of hard economic measures, business strategy goals, or technical strategy goals - while honoring constraints imposed by management or external real-world factors. Typical attributes of projects being analyzed in a _________ process include each project's total expected cost, consumption of scarce resources (human or otherwise) expected timeline and schedule of investment, expected nature, magnitude and timing of benefits to be realized, and relationship or inter-dependencies with other projects in the portfolio.
a. Customer intelligence
b. Power III
c. Pop-up ads
d. Project Portfolio Management

30. _________ consists of the sale of goods or merchandise from a fixed location, such as a department store or kiosk in small or individual lots for direct consumption by the purchaser. _________ may include subordinated services, such as delivery. Purchasers may be individuals or businesses.
a. Warehouse store
b. Thrifting
c. Retailing
d. Charity shop

31. _________ is a form of communication that typically attempts to persuade potential customers to purchase or to consume more of a particular brand of product or service. 'While now central to the contemporary global economy and the reproduction of global production networks, it is only quite recently that _________ has been more than a marginal influence on patterns of sales and production. The formation of modern _________ was intimately bound up with the emergence of new forms of monopoly capitalism around the end of the 19th and beginning of the 20th century as one element in corporate strategies to create, organize and where possible control markets, especially for mass produced consumer goods.
a. AMAX
b. ADTECH
c. ACNielsen
d. Advertising

32. _________ is a magazine, delivering news, analysis and data on marketing and media. The magazine was started as a broadsheet newspaper in Chicago in 1930. Today, its content appears in a print weekly distributed around the world and on many electronic platforms, including: AdAge.com, daily e-mail newsletters called Ad Age Daily, Ad Age's Mediaworks and Ad Age Digital; weekly newsletters such as Madison ' Vine (about branded entertainment) and Ad Age China; podcasts called Why It Matters and various videos.

a. Outsert
b. Advertising Age
c. Ethical Consumer
d. Adweek

33. _________ , according to The American Marketing Association, is 'a planning process designed to assure that all brand contacts received by a customer or prospect for a product, service, or organization are relevant to that person and consistent over time.' (Marketing Power Dictionary)

_________ is a term used to describe a holistic approach to marketing. It aims to ensure consistency of message and the complementary use of media. The concept includes online and offline marketing channels.

a. Integrated marketing communications
b. AMAX
c. ACNielsen
d. ADTECH

34. _________ is one of the four Ps of the marketing mix. The other three aspects are product, promotion, and place. It is also a key variable in microeconomic price allocation theory.

a. Price
b. Competitor indexing
c. Relationship based pricing
d. Pricing

35. An _________ is the manufacturing of a good or service within a category. Although _________ is a broad term for any kind of economic production, in economics and urban planning _________ is a synonym for the secondary sector, which is a type of economic activity involved in the manufacturing of raw materials into goods and products.

There are four key industrial economic sectors: the primary sector, largely raw material extraction industries such as mining and farming; the secondary sector, involving refining, construction, and manufacturing; the tertiary sector, which deals with services (such as law and medicine) and distribution of manufactured goods; and the quaternary sector, a relatively new type of knowledge _________ focusing on technological research, design and development such as computer programming, and biochemistry.

a. Industry
b. AMAX
c. ACNielsen
d. ADTECH

36. _________ refers to messages and related media used to communicate with a market. Those who practice advertising, branding, direct marketing, graphic design, marketing, packaging, promotion, publicity, sponsorship, public relations, sales, sales promotion and online marketing are termed marketing communicators, _________ managers, or more briefly as marcom managers.

a. Merchandising
b. Merchandise
c. Sales promotion
d. Marketing communication

37. _________ is a branch of philosophy which seeks to address questions about morality, such as how a moral outcome can be achieved in a specific situation (applied _________), how moral values should be determined (normative _________), what moral values people actually abide by (descriptive _________), what the fundamental semantic, ontological, and epistemic nature of _________ or morality is (meta-_________), and how moral capacity or moral agency develops and what its nature is (moral psychology.)

Socrates was one of the first Greek philosophers to encourage both scholars and the common citizen to turn their attention from the outside world to the condition of man. In this view, Knowledge having a bearing on human life was placed highest, all other knowledge being secondary.

a. ADTECH
b. ACNielsen
c. Ethics
d. AMAX

38. _________ is an advertisement in which a particular product specifically mentions a competitor by name for the express purpose of showing why the competitor is inferior to the product naming it.

This should not be confused with parody advertisements, where a fictional product is being advertised for the purpose of poking fun at the particular advertisement, nor should it be confused with the use of a coined brand name for the purpose of comparing the product without actually naming an actual competitor. ('Wikipedia tastes better and is less filling than the Encyclopedia Galactica.')

In the 1980s, during what has been referred to as the cola wars, soft-drink manufacturer Pepsi ran a series of advertisements where people, caught on hidden camera, in a blind taste test, chose Pepsi over rival Coca-Cola.

a. Comparative advertising
b. Heavy-up
c. Cost per conversion
d. GL-70

39. In statistics, analysis of variance (_________) is a collection of statistical models, and their associated procedures, in which the observed variance is partitioned into components due to different explanatory variables. In its simplest form _________ gives a statistical test of whether the means of several groups are all equal, and therefore generalizes Student's two-sample t-test to more than two groups.

There are three conceptual classes of such models:

1. Fixed-effects models assumes that the data came from normal populations which may differ only in their means. (Model 1)
2. Random effects models assume that the data describe a hierarchy of different populations whose differences are constrained by the hierarchy. (Model 2)
3. Mixed-effect models describe situations where both fixed and random effects are present. (Model 3)

In practice, there are several types of _________ depending on the number of treatments and the way they are applied to the subjects in the experiment:

- One-way _________ is used to test for differences among two or more independent groups. Typically, however, the one-way _________ is used to test for differences among at least three groups, since the two-group case can be covered by a T-test (Gossett, 1908.)

a. ANOVA
b. AMAX
c. ACNielsen
d. ADTECH

40. A _________ is a formal statement of a set of business goals, the reasons why they are believed attainable, and the plan for reaching those goals. It may also contain background information about the organization or team attempting to reach those goals.

The business goals may be defined for for-profit or for non-profit organizations.

a. Product marketing
b. Logistics management
c. Digital strategy
d. Business plan

41. Founded in 1957, the _________ is one of the largest trade associations of market research and polling professionals. _________ has more than 3,000 members worldwide, representing all segments of the research industry. _________ advances, protects and promotes knowledge, standards, excellence, ethics, professional development and innovation for the global market and opinion research profession.
a. 180SearchAssistant
b. PRSA
c. Marketing Research Association
d. Power III

1. _________ is defined by the American _________ Association as the activity, set of institutions, and processes for creating, communicating, delivering, and exchanging offerings that have value for customers, clients, partners, and society at large. The term developed from the original meaning which referred literally to going to market, as in shopping, or going to a market to sell goods or services.

_________ practice tends to be seen as a creative industry, which includes advertising, distribution and selling.

a. Marketing
b. Customer acquisition management
c. Marketing myopia
d. Product naming

2. Consumer market research is a form of applied sociology that concentrates on understanding the behaviours, whims and preferences, of consumers in a market-based economy, and aims to understand the effects and comparative success of marketing campaigns. The field of consumer _________ as a statistical science was pioneered by Arthur Nielsen with the founding of the ACNielsen Company in 1923 .

Thus _________ is the systematic and objective identification, collection, analysis, and dissemination of information for the purpose of assisting management in decision making related to the identification and solution of problems and opportunities in marketing.

a. Focus group
b. Logit analysis
c. Marketing research process
d. Marketing research

3. _________ is a set of six steps which defines the tasks to be accomplished in conducting a marketing research study. These include problem definition, developing an approach to problem, research design formulation, field work, data preparation and analysis, and report generation and presentation.

a. Preference-rank translation
b. Market analysis
c. Simple random sampling
d. Marketing research process

4. _________ in its literal sense is the process of transformation of local or regional phenomena into global ones. It can be described as a process by which the people of the world are unified into a single society and function together.

This process is a combination of economic, technological, sociocultural and political forces.

a. Globalization
b. 6-3-5 Brainwriting
c. Power III
d. 180SearchAssistant

5. _________ is a term for unprocessed data, it is also known as primary data. It is a relative term _________ can be input to a computer program or used in manual analysis procedures such as gathering statistics from a survey.
a. Chief marketing officer
b. Shoppers Food ' Pharmacy
c. Product manager
d. Raw data

6. Combining Existing _________ Sources with New Primary Data Sources

Imagine that we could get hold of a good collection of surveys taken in earlier years, such as detailed studies about changes going on in this phase and hopefully additional studies in the years to come. Analyzing this data base over time could give us a good picture of what changes actually have taken place in the orientation of the population and of the extent to which new technical concepts did have an impact on subgroups of the population. Furthermore, data archives can help to prepare studies on change over time by monitoring what questions have been asked in earlier years and alerting principal investigators to important questions which should be repeated in planned research projects.

a. 180SearchAssistant
b. 6-3-5 Brainwriting
c. Power III
d. Secondary data

7. In economics, business, retail, and accounting, a _________ is the value of money that has been used up to produce something, and hence is not available for use anymore. In economics, a _________ is an alternative that is given up as a result of a decision. In business, the _________ may be one of acquisition, in which case the amount of money expended to acquire it is counted as _________.
a. Fixed costs
b. Variable cost
c. Cost
d. Transaction cost

8. _________ consists of the processes a company uses to track and organize its contacts with its current and prospective customers. _________ software is used to support these processes; information about customers and customer interactions can be entered, stored and accessed by employees in different company departments. Typical _________ goals are to improve services provided to customers, and to use customer contact information for targeted marketing.

a. Commercialization
b. Product bundling
c. Demand generation
d. Customer relationship management

9. _________ refer to a collection of facts usually collected as the result of experience, observation or experiment or a set of premises. This may consist of numbers, words particularly as measurements or observations of a set of variables. _________ are often viewed as a lowest level of abstraction from which information and knowledge are derived.

a. Data
b. Mean
c. Pearson product-moment correlation coefficient
d. Sample size

10. _________ is a term used to describe a process of preparing and collecting data - for example as part of a process improvement or similar project.

_________ usually takes place early on in an improvement project, and is often formalised through a _________ Plan which often contains the following activity.

1. Pre collection activity - Agree goals, target data, definitions, methods
2. Collection - _________
3. Present Findings - usually involves some form of sorting analysis and/or presentation.

A formal _________ process is necessary as it ensures that data gathered is both defined and accurate and that subsequent decisions based on arguments embodied in the findings are valid . The process provides both a baseline from which to measure from and in certain cases a target on what to improve. Types of _________ 1-By mail questionnaires 2-By personal interview

- Six sigma
- Sampling (statistics)

a. 6-3-5 Brainwriting
b. 180SearchAssistant
c. Power III
d. Data collection

11. Customer _________ consists of the processes a company uses to track and organize its contacts with its current and prospective customers. CRelationship management software is used to support these processes; information about customers and customer interactions can be entered, stored and accessed by employees in different company departments. Typical CRelationship management goals are to improve services provided to customers, and to use customer contact information for targeted marketing.
a. Green marketing
b. Marketing
c. Relationship management
d. Product bundling

12. A personal and cultural _________ is a relative ethic _________, an assumption upon which implementation can be extrapolated. A _________ system is a set of consistent _________s and measures that is soo not true. A principle _________ is a foundation upon which other _________s and measures of integrity are based.
a. Value
b. Package-on-Package
c. Supreme Court of the United States
d. Perceptual maps

13. _________ is a marketing term, and involves evaluating the situation and trends in a particular company's market. _________ is often called the 'three c's', which refers to the three major elements that must be studied:

- Customers
- Costs
- Competition

The number of 'c's' is sometimes extended to four, five, or even six, with 'Collaboration', 'Company', and 'Competitive advantage'.

- Marketing mix
- SWOT analysis

.

a. Power III
b. 180SearchAssistant
c. 6-3-5 Brainwriting
d. Situation analysis

14. Competitiveness is a comparative concept of the ability and performance of a firm, sub-sector or country to sell and supply goods and/or services in a given market. Although widely used in economics and business management, the usefulness of the concept, particularly in the context of national competitiveness, is vigorously disputed by economists, such as Paul Krugman .

The term may also be applied to markets, where it is used to refer to the extent to which the market structure may be regarded as perfectly _________.

a. Customs union
b. Geographical pricing
c. Free trade zone
d. Competitive

15. The _________ is the major entity that is being analyzed in the study. It is the 'what' or 'whom' that is being studied. In social science research, the most typical units of analysis are individual people.
a. AMAX
b. Unit of analysis
c. ADTECH
d. ACNielsen

16. _________s are used in open sentences. For instance, in the formula x + 1 = 5, x is a _________ which represents an 'unknown' number. _________s are often represented by letters of the Roman alphabet, or those of other alphabets, such as Greek, and use other special symbols.
a. Personalization
b. Book of business
c. Variable
d. Quantitative

17. _________, a business term, is a measure of how products and services supplied by a company meet or surpass customer expectation. It is seen as a key performance indicator within business and is part of the four perspectives of a Balanced Scorecard.

In a competitive marketplace where businesses compete for customers, _________ is seen as a key differentiator and increasingly has become a key element of business strategy.

a. Supplier diversity
b. Psychological pricing
c. Customer base
d. Customer satisfaction

18. _________ describes data and characteristics about the population or phenomenon being studied. _________ answers the questions who, what, where, when and how.

Although the data description is factual, accurate and systematic, the research cannot describe what caused a situation.

a. Power III
b. Two-tailed test
c. Descriptive research
d. Sampling error

19. _________ is a type of research conducted because a problem has not been clearly defined. _________ helps determine the best research design, data collection method and selection of subjects. Given its fundamental nature, _________ often concludes that a perceived problem does not actually exist.

a. IDDEA
b. Exploratory research
c. Intent scale translation
d. ACNielsen

20. A _________ is a form of qualitative research in which a group of people are asked about their attitude towards a product, service, concept, advertisement, idea, or packaging. Questions are asked in an interactive group setting where participants are free to talk with other group members.

Ernest Dichter originated the idea of having a 'group therapy' for products and this process is what became known as a _________.

a. Cross tabulation
b. Logit analysis
c. Focus group
d. Marketing research process

21. A number of different _________s are indicated below.

- Randomized controlled trial
  - Double-blind randomized trial
  - Single-blind randomized trial
  - Non-blind trial
- Nonrandomized trial (quasi-experiment)
  - Interrupted time series design (measures on a sample or a series of samples from the same population are obtained several times before and after a manipulated event or a naturally occurring event) - considered a type of quasi-experiment

- Cohort study
  - Prospective cohort
  - Retrospective cohort
  - Time series study
- Case-control study
  - Nested case-control study
- Cross-sectional study
  - Community survey (a type of cross-sectional study)

When choosing a _________, many factors must be taken into account. Different types of studies are subject to different types of bias. For example, recall bias is likely to occur in cross-sectional or case-control studies where subjects are asked to recall exposure to risk factors.

a. Longitudinal studies
b. Study design
c. 180SearchAssistant
d. Power III

22. _________ a research method involving the use of questionnaires and/or statistical surveys to gather data about people and their thoughts and behaviours.

a. T-test
b. Control chart
c. Z-test
d. Survey research

23. Sampling is the use of a subset of the population to represent the whole population. Probability sampling, or random sampling, is a sampling technique in which the probability of getting any particular sample may be calculated. _________ does not meet this criterion and should be used with caution.

a. Power III
b. Snowball sampling
c. Nonprobability sampling
d. Quota sampling

24. _________ is a way of expressing knowledge or belief that an event will occur or has occurred. In mathematics the concept has been given an exact meaning in _________ theory, that is used extensively in such areas of study as mathematics, statistics, finance, gambling, science, and philosophy to draw conclusions about the likelihood of potential events and the underlying mechanics of complex systems.

a. Linear regression
b. Heteroskedastic
c. Data
d. Probability

25. The _________ of a statistical sample is the number of observations that constitute it. It is typically denoted n, a positive integer (natural number.)

Typically, all else being equal, a larger _________ leads to increased precision in estimates of various properties of the population.

a. Heteroskedastic
b. Data
c. Frequency distribution
d. Sample size

26. _________ is that part of statistical practice concerned with the selection of individual observations intended to yield some knowledge about a population of concern, especially for the purposes of statistical inference. Each observation measures one or more properties (weight, location, etc.) of an observable entity enumerated to distinguish objects or individuals.

a. Richard Buckminster 'Bucky' Fuller
b. Sports Marketing Group
c. AStore
d. Sampling

27. A _________ is a research instrument consisting of a series of questions and other prompts for the purpose of gathering information from respondents. Although they are often designed for statistical analysis of the responses, this is not always the case. The _________ was invented by Sir Francis Galton.

a. Mystery shoppers
b. Mystery shopping
c. Questionnaire
d. Market research

28. _________ is a form of communication that typically attempts to persuade potential customers to purchase or to consume more of a particular brand of product or service. 'While now central to the contemporary global economy and the reproduction of global production networks, it is only quite recently that _________ has been more than a marginal influence on patterns of sales and production. The formation of modern _________ was intimately bound up with the emergence of new forms of monopoly capitalism around the end of the 19th and beginning of the 20th century as one element in corporate strategies to create, organize and where possible control markets, especially for mass produced consumer goods.

a. ACNielsen
b. ADTECH
c. AMAX
d. Advertising

1. _________ is a form of communication that typically attempts to persuade potential customers to purchase or to consume more of a particular brand of product or service. 'While now central to the contemporary global economy and the reproduction of global production networks, it is only quite recently that _________ has been more than a marginal influence on patterns of sales and production. The formation of modern _________ was intimately bound up with the emergence of new forms of monopoly capitalism around the end of the 19th and beginning of the 20th century as one element in corporate strategies to create, organize and where possible control markets, especially for mass produced consumer goods.

a. Advertising
b. ADTECH
c. AMAX
d. ACNielsen

2. A personal and cultural _________ is a relative ethic _________, an assumption upon which implementation can be extrapolated. A _________ system is a set of consistent _________s and measures that is soo not true. A principle _________ is a foundation upon which other _________s and measures of integrity are based.

a. Supreme Court of the United States
b. Package-on-Package
c. Perceptual maps
d. Value

3. _________ refer to a collection of facts usually collected as the result of experience, observation or experiment or a set of premises. This may consist of numbers, words particularly as measurements or observations of a set of variables. _________ are often viewed as a lowest level of abstraction from which information and knowledge are derived.

a. Pearson product-moment correlation coefficient
b. Sample size
c. Data
d. Mean

4. _________ is a process of gathering, modeling, and transforming data with the goal of highlighting useful information, suggesting conclusions, and supporting decision making. _________ has multiple facets and approaches, encompassing diverse techniques under a variety of names, in different business, science, and social science domains.

Data mining is a particular _________ technique that focuses on modeling and knowledge discovery for predictive rather than purely descriptive purposes.

a. 180SearchAssistant
b. 6-3-5 Brainwriting
c. Power III
d. Data analysis

5. The _________ is an English-language international daily newspaper published by Dow Jones ' Company in New York City with Asian and European editions. As of 2007, It has a worldwide daily circulation of more than 2 million, with approximately 931,000 paying online subscribers. It was the largest-circulation newspaper in the United States until November 2003, when it was surpassed by USA Today.

a. 6-3-5 Brainwriting
b. 180SearchAssistant
c. Power III
d. Wall Street Journal

6. _________ is defined by the American _________ Association as the activity, set of institutions, and processes for creating, communicating, delivering, and exchanging offerings that have value for customers, clients, partners, and society at large. The term developed from the original meaning which referred literally to going to market, as in shopping, or going to a market to sell goods or services.

_________ practice tends to be seen as a creative industry, which includes advertising, distribution and selling.

a. Marketing myopia
b. Customer acquisition management
c. Product naming
d. Marketing

7. A _________ is a type of website, usually maintained by an individual with regular entries of commentary, descriptions of events, or other material such as graphics or video. Entries are commonly displayed in reverse-chronological order. '_________' can also be used as a verb, meaning to maintain or add content to a _________.

a. 180SearchAssistant
b. Blog
c. 6-3-5 Brainwriting
d. Power III

8. The terms '_________' and 'independent variable' are used in similar but subtly different ways in mathematics and statistics as part of the standard terminology in those subjects. They are used to distinguish between two types of quantities being considered, separating them into those available at the start of a process and those being created by it, where the latter (_________s) are dependent on the former (independent variables.)

In traditional calculus, a function is defined as a relation between two terms called variables because their values vary.

a. Power III
b. 180SearchAssistant
c. Field experiment
d. Dependent variable

9. _________s are used in open sentences. For instance, in the formula x + 1 = 5, x is a _________ which represents an 'unknown' number. _________s are often represented by letters of the Roman alphabet, or those of other alphabets, such as Greek, and use other special symbols.
a. Variable
b. Quantitative
c. Book of business
d. Personalization

10. _________ is a type of research conducted because a problem has not been clearly defined. _________ helps determine the best research design, data collection method and selection of subjects. Given its fundamental nature, _________ often concludes that a perceived problem does not actually exist.
a. Exploratory research
b. Intent scale translation
c. ACNielsen
d. IDDEA

11. Consumer market research is a form of applied sociology that concentrates on understanding the behaviours, whims and preferences, of consumers in a market-based economy, and aims to understand the effects and comparative success of marketing campaigns. The field of consumer _________ as a statistical science was pioneered by Arthur Nielsen with the founding of the ACNielsen Company in 1923 .

Thus _________ is the systematic and objective identification, collection, analysis, and dissemination of information for the purpose of assisting management in decision making related to the identification and solution of problems and opportunities in marketing.

a. Focus group
b. Marketing research process
c. Logit analysis
d. Marketing research

12. In statistics, the _________ is a common measure of the correlation (linear dependence) between two variables X and Y. It is very widely used in the sciences as a measure of the strength of linear dependence between two variables, giving a value somewhere between +1 and -1 inclusive. It was first introduced by Francis Galton in the 1880s, and named after Karl Pearson.

In accordance with the usual convention, when calculated for an entire population, the Pearson product-moment correlation is typically designated by the analogous Greek letter, which in this case is ρ .

a. Control chart
b. Pearson product-moment correlation coefficient
c. Standard deviation
d. Median

13. In probability theory and statistics, _________ indicates the strength and direction of a linear relationship between two random variables. That is in contrast with the usage of the term in colloquial speech, denoting any relationship, not necessarily linear. In general statistical usage, _________ or co-relation refers to the departure of two random variables from independence.

a. Mean
b. Frequency distribution
c. Probability
d. Correlation

14. The _________ and the null hypothesis are the two rival hypotheses whose likelihoods are compared by a statistical hypothesis test. Usually the _________ is the possibility that an observed effect is genuine and the null hypothesis is the rival possibility that it has resulted from chance.

The classical (or frequentist) approach is to calculate the probability that the observed effect (or one more extreme) will occur if the null hypothesis is true.

a. Alternative hypothesis
b. ACNielsen
c. Analysis of variance
d. Interval estimation

15. 'Speaking generally, properties are those physical quantities which directly describe the physical attributes of the system; _________s are those combinations of the properties which suffice to determine the response of the system. Properties can have all sorts of dimensions, depending upon the system being considered; _________s are dimensionless, or have the dimension of time or its reciprocal.'

The term can also be used in engineering contexts, however, as it is typically used in the physical sciences.

When the terms formal _________ and actual _________ are used, they generally correspond with the definitions used in computer science.

a. 6-3-5 Brainwriting
b. Power III
c. 180SearchAssistant
d. Parameter

16. In statistical hypothesis testing, the _________ formally describes some aspect of the statistical behaviour of a set of data; this description is treated as valid unless the actual behaviour of the data contradicts this assumption. Thus, the _________ is contrasted against another hypothesis. Statistical hypothesis testing is used to make a decision about whether the data contradicts the _________: this is called significance testing.

a. Statistical hypothesis test
b. Variance
c. Standard score
d. Null Hypothesis

17. The loyalty business model is a business model used in strategic management in which company resources are employed so as to increase the loyalty of customers and other stakeholders in the expectation that corporate objectives will be met or surpassed. A typical example of this type of model is: quality of product or service leads to customer satisfaction, which leads to _________, which leads to profitability.

Fredrick Reichheld (1996) expanded the loyalty business model beyond customers and employees.

a. Power III
b. 6-3-5 Brainwriting
c. 180SearchAssistant
d. Customer loyalty

18. _________, a business term, is a measure of how products and services supplied by a company meet or surpass customer expectation. It is seen as a key performance indicator within business and is part of the four perspectives of a Balanced Scorecard.

In a competitive marketplace where businesses compete for customers, _________ is seen as a key differentiator and increasingly has become a key element of business strategy.

a. Supplier diversity
b. Customer satisfaction
c. Customer base
d. Psychological pricing

1. In economics, an externality or spillover of an economic transaction is an impact on a party that is not directly involved in the transaction. In such a case, prices do not reflect the full costs or benefits in production or consumption of a product or service. A positive impact is called an _________ benefit, while a negative impact is called an _________ cost.

a. External
b. ACNielsen
c. ADTECH
d. AMAX

2. Combining Existing _________ Sources with New Primary Data Sources

Imagine that we could get hold of a good collection of surveys taken in earlier years, such as detailed studies about changes going on in this phase and hopefully additional studies in the years to come. Analyzing this data base over time could give us a good picture of what changes actually have taken place in the orientation of the population and of the extent to which new technical concepts did have an impact on subgroups of the population. Furthermore, data archives can help to prepare studies on change over time by monitoring what questions have been asked in earlier years and alerting principal investigators to important questions which should be repeated in planned research projects.

a. Power III
b. 6-3-5 Brainwriting
c. 180SearchAssistant
d. Secondary data

3. _________ consists of the processes a company uses to track and organize its contacts with its current and prospective customers. _________ software is used to support these processes; information about customers and customer interactions can be entered, stored and accessed by employees in different company departments. Typical _________ goals are to improve services provided to customers, and to use customer contact information for targeted marketing.

a. Demand generation
b. Product bundling
c. Commercialization
d. Customer relationship management

4. _________ refer to a collection of facts usually collected as the result of experience, observation or experiment or a set of premises. This may consist of numbers, words particularly as measurements or observations of a set of variables. _________ are often viewed as a lowest level of abstraction from which information and knowledge are derived.

a. Pearson product-moment correlation coefficient
b. Sample size
c. Data
d. Mean

5. Customer _________ consists of the processes a company uses to track and organize its contacts with its current and prospective customers. CRelationship management software is used to support these processes; information about customers and customer interactions can be entered, stored and accessed by employees in different company departments. Typical CRelationship management goals are to improve services provided to customers, and to use customer contact information for targeted marketing.
a. Product bundling
b. Relationship management
c. Marketing
d. Green marketing

6. A personal and cultural _________ is a relative ethic _________, an assumption upon which implementation can be extrapolated. A _________ system is a set of consistent _________s and measures that is soo not true. A principle _________ is a foundation upon which other _________s and measures of integrity are based.
a. Perceptual maps
b. Value
c. Supreme Court of the United States
d. Package-on-Package

7. Procter is a surname, and may also refer to:

- Bryan Waller Procter (pseud. Barry Cornwall), English poet
- Goodwin Procter, American law firm
- _________, consumer products multinational

.

a. Procter ' Gamble
b. Black PRies
c. Flyer
d. Convergent

8. _________ is a form of marketing developed from direct response marketing campaigns conducted in the 1970's and 1980's which emphasizes customer retention and satisfaction, rather than a dominant focus on 'point of sale' transactions.

_________ differs from other forms of marketing in that it recognizes the long term value to the firm of keeping customers, as opposed to direct or 'Intrusion' marketing, which focuses upon acquisition of new clients by targeting majority demographics based upon prospective client lists.

_________ refers to long-term and mutually beneficial arrangement wherein both buyer and seller focus on value enhancement through the certain of more satisfying exchange.This approach attempts to transcend the simple purchase exchange process with customer to make more meaningful and richer contact by providing a more holistic, personalized purchase, and use orn consumption experience to create stronger ties.

a. Relationship marketing
b. Guerrilla Marketing
c. Global marketing
d. Diversity marketing

9. _________ is defined by the American _________ Association as the activity, set of institutions, and processes for creating, communicating, delivering, and exchanging offerings that have value for customers, clients, partners, and society at large. The term developed from the original meaning which referred literally to going to market, as in shopping, or going to a market to sell goods or services.

_________ practice tends to be seen as a creative industry, which includes advertising, distribution and selling.

a. Product naming
b. Customer acquisition management
c. Marketing
d. Marketing myopia

10. Consumer market research is a form of applied sociology that concentrates on understanding the behaviours, whims and preferences, of consumers in a market-based economy, and aims to understand the effects and comparative success of marketing campaigns. The field of consumer _________ as a statistical science was pioneered by Arthur Nielsen with the founding of the ACNielsen Company in 1923 .

Thus _________ is the systematic and objective identification, collection, analysis, and dissemination of information for the purpose of assisting management in decision making related to the identification and solution of problems and opportunities in marketing.

a. Marketing research process
b. Focus group
c. Logit analysis
d. Marketing research

11. _________ is a set of six steps which defines the tasks to be accomplished in conducting a marketing research study. These include problem definition, developing an approach to problem, research design formulation, field work, data preparation and analysis, and report generation and presentation.
a. Preference-rank translation
b. Simple random sampling
c. Market analysis
d. Marketing research process

12. _________ is a term for unprocessed data, it is also known as primary data. It is a relative term _________ can be input to a computer program or used in manual analysis procedures such as gathering statistics from a survey.
a. Raw data
b. Product manager
c. Shoppers Food ' Pharmacy
d. Chief marketing officer

13. In economics, business, retail, and accounting, a _________ is the value of money that has been used up to produce something, and hence is not available for use anymore. In economics, a _________ is an alternative that is given up as a result of a decision. In business, the _________ may be one of acquisition, in which case the amount of money expended to acquire it is counted as _________.
a. Cost
b. Variable cost
c. Transaction cost
d. Fixed costs

14. _________ is a term used to describe a process of preparing and collecting data - for example as part of a process improvement or similar project.

_________ usually takes place early on in an improvement project, and is often formalised through a _________ Plan which often contains the following activity.

1. Pre collection activity - Agree goals, target data, definitions, methods
2. Collection - _________
3. Present Findings - usually involves some form of sorting analysis and/or presentation.

A formal _________ process is necessary as it ensures that data gathered is both defined and accurate and that subsequent decisions based on arguments embodied in the findings are valid . The process provides both a baseline from which to measure from and in certain cases a target on what to improve. Types of _________ 1-By mail questionnaires 2-By personal interview

- Six sigma
- Sampling (statistics)

.

a. 6-3-5 Brainwriting
b. Power III
c. 180SearchAssistant
d. Data collection

15. _________ in organizations and public policy is both the organizational process of creating and maintaining a plan; and the psychological process of thinking about the activities required to create a desired goal on some scale. As such, it is a fundamental property of intelligent behavior. This thought process is essential to the creation and refinement of a plan, or integration of it with other plans, that is, it combines forecasting of developments with the preparation of scenarios of how to react to them.

a. 180SearchAssistant
b. 6-3-5 Brainwriting
c. Planning
d. Power III

16. _________ is a standard point of view or personal prejudice. especially when the tendency interferes with the ability to be impartial, unprejudiced, or objective. The term _________ed is used to describe an action, judgment, or other outcome influenced by a prejudged perspective.

a. 6-3-5 Brainwriting
b. 180SearchAssistant
c. Power III
d. Bias

17. In accounting, _________ has a very specific meaning. It is an outflow of cash or other valuable assets from a person or company to another person or company. This outflow of cash is generally one side of a trade for products or services that have equal or better current or future value to the buyer than to the seller.

a. ACNielsen
b. Expense
c. AMAX
d. ADTECH

18. _________s are used in open sentences. For instance, in the formula x + 1 = 5, x is a _________ which represents an 'unknown' number. _________s are often represented by letters of the Roman alphabet, or those of other alphabets, such as Greek, and use other special symbols.

a. Book of business
b. Personalization
c. Quantitative
d. Variable

19. An _________ is the manufacturing of a good or service within a category. Although _________ is a broad term for any kind of economic production, in economics and urban planning _________ is a synonym for the secondary sector, which is a type of economic activity involved in the manufacturing of raw materials into goods and products.

There are four key industrial economic sectors: the primary sector, largely raw material extraction industries such as mining and farming; the secondary sector, involving refining, construction, and manufacturing; the tertiary sector, which deals with services (such as law and medicine) and distribution of manufactured goods; and the quaternary sector, a relatively new type of knowledge _________ focusing on technological research, design and development such as computer programming, and biochemistry.

a. Industry
b. ADTECH
c. ACNielsen
d. AMAX

20. The _________ or _________ is used by business and government to classify and measure economic activity in Canada, Mexico and the United States. It has largely replaced the older Standard Industrial Classification system; however, certain government departments and agencies, such as the U.S. Securities and Exchange Commission (SEC), still use the SIC codes.

The _________ numbering system is a six-digit code.

a. 180SearchAssistant
b. Power III
c. North American Industry Classification System
d. 6-3-5 Brainwriting

21. The United States _________ is the government agency that is responsible for the United States Census. It also gathers other national demographic and economic data.
a. 6-3-5 Brainwriting
b. Power III
c. Census Bureau
d. 180SearchAssistant

22. The United States _________ is the Cabinet department of the United States government concerned with promoting economic growth. It was originally created as the United States _________ and Labor on February 14, 1903. It was subsequently renamed to the _________ on March 4, 1913, and its bureaus and agencies specializing in labor were transferred to the new Department of Labor.
a. Power III
b. 180SearchAssistant
c. 6-3-5 Brainwriting
d. Department of Commerce

23. The _________ is the Cabinet department of the United States government concerned with promoting economic growth. It was originally created as the _________ and Labor on February 14, 1903. It was subsequently renamed to the Department of Commerce on March 4, 1913, and its bureaus and agencies specializing in labor were transferred to the new Department of Labor.
a. United States Department of Commerce
b. ACNielsen
c. AMAX
d. ADTECH

24. A _________ is a structured collection of records or data that is stored in a computer system. The structure is achieved by organizing the data according to a _________ model. The model in most common use today is the relational model.
a. 180SearchAssistant
b. 6-3-5 Brainwriting
c. Power III
d. Database

25. _________ or _________ data refers to selected population characteristics as used in government, marketing or opinion research, or the _________ profiles used in such research. Note the distinction from the term 'demography' Commonly-used _________ include race, age, income, disabilities, mobility (in terms of travel time to work or number of vehicles available), educational attainment, home ownership, employment status, and even location.

a. African Americans
b. Albert Einstein
c. AStore
d. Demographic

26. A _________ is a documented investigation of a Market that is used to inform a firm's planning activities particularly around decision of: inventory, purchase, work force expansion/contraction, facility expansion, purchases of capital equipment, promotional activities, and many other aspects of a company.

Not all managers are asked to conduct a _________, but all managers must make decisions using _________ data and understand how the data was derived. So all managers need a reasonable understanding of the tools most used for making sales forecasts and analyzing markets.

a. Preference regression
b. Market Analysis
c. Simple random sampling
d. Cross tabulation

27. _________ refers to the methods, practices and operations conducted to promote and sustain certain categories of commercial activity. The term is understood to have different specific meanings depending on the context. Merchandise is a sale goods at a store

In marketing, one of the definitions of _________ is the practice in which the brand or image from one product or service is used to sell another.

a. Marketing communication
b. Word of mouth
c. Merchandising
d. New Media Strategies

28. _________ is a mathematical science pertaining to the collection, analysis, interpretation or explanation, and presentation of data. It also provides tools for prediction and forecasting based on data. It is applicable to a wide variety of academic disciplines, from the natural and social sciences to the humanities, government and business.

a. Null hypothesis
b. Statistics
c. Type I error
d. Median

29. Competitiveness is a comparative concept of the ability and performance of a firm, sub-sector or country to sell and supply goods and/or services in a given market. Although widely used in economics and business management, the usefulness of the concept, particularly in the context of national competitiveness, is vigorously disputed by economists, such as Paul Krugman .

The term may also be applied to markets, where it is used to refer to the extent to which the market structure may be regarded as perfectly _________.

a. Geographical pricing
b. Competitive
c. Free trade zone
d. Customs union

30. In statistics, the _________ is a common measure of the correlation (linear dependence) between two variables X and Y. It is very widely used in the sciences as a measure of the strength of linear dependence between two variables, giving a value somewhere between +1 and -1 inclusive. It was first introduced by Francis Galton in the 1880s, and named after Karl Pearson.

In accordance with the usual convention, when calculated for an entire population, the Pearson product-moment correlation is typically designated by the analogous Greek letter, which in this case is ρ .

a. Pearson product-moment correlation coefficient
b. Median
c. Control chart
d. Standard deviation

31. In probability theory and statistics, _________ indicates the strength and direction of a linear relationship between two random variables. That is in contrast with the usage of the term in colloquial speech, denoting any relationship, not necessarily linear. In general statistical usage, _________ or co-relation refers to the departure of two random variables from independence.

a. Probability
b. Frequency distribution
c. Mean
d. Correlation

32. _________ is a broad label that refers to any individuals or households that use goods and services generated within the economy. The concept of a _________ is used in different contexts, so that the usage and significance of the term may vary.

A _________ is a person who uses any product or service.

a. 6-3-5 Brainwriting
b. 180SearchAssistant
c. Power III
d. Consumer

33. _________ is a radio audience research company in the United States which collects listener data on radio audiences similar to that collected by Nielsen Media Research on television audiences. It was founded as American Research Bureau by Jim Seiler in 1949 and became bi-coastal by merging with L.A. based Coffin, Cooper and Clay in the early 1950s. ARB's initial business was the collection of television broadcast ratings exclusively.
a. American Heart Association
b. American Cancer Society
c. Access Commerce
d. Arbitron

34. _________ is an American firm that measures media audiences, including television, radio, theatre films (via the AMC MAP program) and newspapers. _________, headquartered in New York City and operating primarily from Chicago, is best-known for the Nielsen Ratings, a measurement of television viewership.

_________, the preeminent media research company in the world, began as a division of ACNielsen, a marketing research firm.

a. Nielsen Media Research
b. CoolBrands
c. Hennes ' Mauritz
d. Green Earth Market

35. _________ is an advertisement in which a particular product specifically mentions a competitor by name for the express purpose of showing why the competitor is inferior to the product naming it.

This should not be confused with parody advertisements, where a fictional product is being advertised for the purpose of poking fun at the particular advertisement, nor should it be confused with the use of a coined brand name for the purpose of comparing the product without actually naming an actual competitor. ('Wikipedia tastes better and is less filling than the Encyclopedia Galactica.')

In the 1980s, during what has been referred to as the cola wars, soft-drink manufacturer Pepsi ran a series of advertisements where people, caught on hidden camera, in a blind taste test, chose Pepsi over rival Coca-Cola.

a. GL-70
b. Heavy-up
c. Comparative advertising
d. Cost per conversion

36. The general definition of an _________ is an evaluation of a person, organization, system, process, project or product. _________s are performed to ascertain the validity and reliability of information; also to provide an assessment of a system's internal control. The goal of an _________ is to express an opinion on the person/organization/system (etc) in question, under evaluation based on work done on a test basis.

a. ACNielsen
b. ADTECH
c. Audit
d. AMAX

1. _________ is a type of research conducted because a problem has not been clearly defined. _________ helps determine the best research design, data collection method and selection of subjects. Given its fundamental nature, _________ often concludes that a perceived problem does not actually exist.
   a. Intent scale translation
   b. IDDEA
   c. ACNielsen
   d. Exploratory research

2. _________ is a field of inquiry that crosscuts disciplines and subject matters . _________ers aim to gather an in-depth understanding of human behavior and the reasons that govern such behavior. The discipline investigates the why and how of decision making, not just what, where, when.
   a. Power III
   b. 6-3-5 Brainwriting
   c. 180SearchAssistant
   d. Qualitative research

3. A personal and cultural _________ is a relative ethic _________, an assumption upon which implementation can be extrapolated. A _________ system is a set of consistent _________s and measures that is soo not true. A principle _________ is a foundation upon which other _________s and measures of integrity are based.
   a. Supreme Court of the United States
   b. Value
   c. Perceptual maps
   d. Package-on-Package

4. A _________ attribute is one that exists in a range of magnitudes, and can therefore be measured. Measurements of any particular _________ property are expressed as a specific quantity, referred to as a unit, multiplied by a number. Examples of physical quantities are distance, mass, and time.
   a. Dolly Dimples
   b. Lifestyle city
   c. BeyondROI
   d. Quantitative

5. _________ refer to a collection of facts usually collected as the result of experience, observation or experiment or a set of premises. This may consist of numbers, words particularly as measurements or observations of a set of variables. _________ are often viewed as a lowest level of abstraction from which information and knowledge are derived.

a. Mean
b. Sample size
c. Pearson product-moment correlation coefficient
d. Data

6. _________ is a process of gathering, modeling, and transforming data with the goal of highlighting useful information, suggesting conclusions, and supporting decision making. _________ has multiple facets and approaches, encompassing diverse techniques under a variety of names, in different business, science, and social science domains.

Data mining is a particular _________ technique that focuses on modeling and knowledge discovery for predictive rather than purely descriptive purposes.

a. 6-3-5 Brainwriting
b. 180SearchAssistant
c. Power III
d. Data analysis

7. A number of different _________s are indicated below.

- Randomized controlled trial
  - Double-blind randomized trial
  - Single-blind randomized trial
  - Non-blind trial
- Nonrandomized trial (quasi-experiment)
  - Interrupted time series design (measures on a sample or a series of samples from the same population are obtained several times before and after a manipulated event or a naturally occurring event) - considered a type of quasi-experiment

- Cohort study
  - Prospective cohort
  - Retrospective cohort
  - Time series study
- Case-control study
  - Nested case-control study
- Cross-sectional study
  - Community survey (a type of cross-sectional study)

When choosing a _________, many factors must be taken into account. Different types of studies are subject to different types of bias. For example, recall bias is likely to occur in cross-sectional or case-control studies where subjects are asked to recall exposure to risk factors.

a. Study design
b. Power III
c. Longitudinal studies
d. 180SearchAssistant

8. _________ is an independent technology and market research company that provides its clients with advice about technology's impact on business and consumers. _________ has four research centers in the US: Cambridge, Massachusetts; Foster City, California; Washington, D.C.; and Westport, Connecticut. It also has four European research centers in Amsterdam, Frankfurt, London, and Paris.

a. Mapinfo
b. Forrester Research
c. BigMachines
d. GlobalSpec

9. The _________ of a statistical sample is the number of observations that constitute it. It is typically denoted n, a positive integer (natural number.)

Typically, all else being equal, a larger _________ leads to increased precision in estimates of various properties of the population.

a. Heteroskedastic
b. Frequency distribution
c. Sample size
d. Data

10. A _________ is a form of qualitative research in which a group of people are asked about their attitude towards a product, service, concept, advertisement, idea, or packaging. Questions are asked in an interactive group setting where participants are free to talk with other group members.

Ernest Dichter originated the idea of having a 'group therapy' for products and this process is what became known as a _________.

a. Marketing research process
b. Cross tabulation
c. Logit analysis
d. Focus group

11. An _________ is one type of focus group, and is a sub-set of online research methods.

A moderator invites prescreened, qualified respondents who represent the target of interest to log on to conferencing software at a pre-arranged time and to take part in an _________. Some researchers will offer incentives for participating but this raises a number of ethical questions.

a. Intangibility
b. Online focus group
c. Automated surveys
d. Engagement

12. _________ is defined by communication scholars in numerous ways, usually describing participants who are dependent upon one another and have a shared history. Communication channels, the conceptualization of mediums that carry messages from sender to receiver, take two distinct forms: direct and indirect.

Direct channels are obvious and easily recognized by the receiver.

a. ADTECH
b. ACNielsen
c. AMAX
d. Interpersonal communication

13. _________ in organizations and public policy is both the organizational process of creating and maintaining a plan; and the psychological process of thinking about the activities required to create a desired goal on some scale. As such, it is a fundamental property of intelligent behavior. This thought process is essential to the creation and refinement of a plan, or integration of it with other plans, that is, it combines forecasting of developments with the preparation of scenarios of how to react to them.

a. Planning
b. Power III
c. 180SearchAssistant
d. 6-3-5 Brainwriting

14. _________ is that part of statistical practice concerned with the selection of individual observations intended to yield some knowledge about a population of concern, especially for the purposes of statistical inference. Each observation measures one or more properties (weight, location, etc.) of an observable entity enumerated to distinguish objects or individuals.

a. Sports Marketing Group
b. Richard Buckminster 'Bucky' Fuller
c. AStore
d. Sampling

15. _________ is a methodology in the social sciences for studying the content of communication. Earl Babbie defines it as 'the study of recorded human communications, such as books, websites, paintings and laws.' It is most commonly used by researchers in the social sciences to analyze recorded transcripts of interviews with participants.

_________ is also considered a scholarly methodology in the humanities by which texts are studied as to authorship, authenticity, of meaning.

a. 180SearchAssistant
b. 6-3-5 Brainwriting
c. Content analysis
d. Power III

16. _________ is a genre of writing that uses fieldwork to provide a descriptive study of human societies. _________ presents the results of a holistic research method founded on the idea that a system's properties cannot necessarily be accurately understood independently of each other. The genre has both formal and historical connections to travel writing and colonial office reports.

a. ACNielsen
b. Ethnography
c. AMAX
d. ADTECH

17. _________ is either an activity of a living being (such as a human), consisting of receiving knowledge of the outside world through the senses, or the recording of data using scientific instruments. The term may also refer to any datum collected during this activity.

The scientific method requires _________s of nature to formulate and test hypotheses.

a. ACNielsen
b. AMAX
c. ADTECH
d. Observation

18. _________ is a broad label that refers to any individuals or households that use goods and services generated within the economy. The concept of a _________ is used in different contexts, so that the usage and significance of the term may vary.

A _________ is a person who uses any product or service.

a. 180SearchAssistant
b. 6-3-5 Brainwriting
c. Consumer
d. Power III

19. _________ is the study of when, why, how, where and what people do or do not buy products. It blends elements from psychology, sociology,social psychology, anthropology and economics. It attempts to understand the buyer decision making process, both individually and in groups. It studies characteristics of individual consumers such as demographics and behavioural variables in an attempt to understand people's wants. It also tries to assess influences on the consumer from groups such as family, friends, reference groups, and society in general.

a. Multidimensional scaling
b. Communal marketing
c. Consumer behavior
d. Consumer confidence

20. _________ is a term developed by Eric von Hippel in 1986. His definition for _________ is:

1. _________s face needs that will be general in a marketplace - but face them months or years before the bulk of that marketplace encounters them, and
2. _________s are positioned to benefit significantly by obtaining a solution to those needs.

In other words: _________s are users of a product that currently experience needs still unknown to the public and who also benefit greatly if they obtain a solution to these needs.

The _________ Method is a market research tool that may be used by companies and / or individuals seeking to develop breakthrough products. _________ methodology was originally developed by Dr. Eric von Hippel of the Massachusetts Institute of Technology (MIT) and first described in the July 1986 issue of the Journal of Management Science.

a. Power III
b. 180SearchAssistant
c. Lead user
d. 6-3-5 Brainwriting

21. The loyalty business model is a business model used in strategic management in which company resources are employed so as to increase the loyalty of customers and other stakeholders in the expectation that corporate objectives will be met or surpassed. A typical example of this type of model is: quality of product or service leads to customer satisfaction, which leads to _________, which leads to profitability.

Fredrick Reichheld (1996) expanded the loyalty business model beyond customers and employees.

a. 6-3-5 Brainwriting
b. Customer loyalty
c. Power III
d. 180SearchAssistant

22. _________ is a common word game involving an exchange of words that are associated together.

Once an original word has been chosen, usually randomly or arbitrarily, a player will find a word that they associate with it and make it known to all the players, usually by saying it aloud or writing it down as the next item on a list of words so far used. The next player must then do the same with this previous word.

a. Word association
b. 6-3-5 Brainwriting
c. 180SearchAssistant
d. Power III

23. In statistics, the _________ is a common measure of the correlation (linear dependence) between two variables X and Y. It is very widely used in the sciences as a measure of the strength of linear dependence between two variables, giving a value somewhere between +1 and -1 inclusive. It was first introduced by Francis Galton in the 1880s, and named after Karl Pearson.

In accordance with the usual convention, when calculated for an entire population, the Pearson product-moment correlation is typically designated by the analogous Greek letter, which in this case is ρ .

a. Control chart
b. Median
c. Standard deviation
d. Pearson product-moment correlation coefficient

24. In probability theory and statistics, _________ indicates the strength and direction of a linear relationship between two random variables. That is in contrast with the usage of the term in colloquial speech, denoting any relationship, not necessarily linear. In general statistical usage, _________ or co-relation refers to the departure of two random variables from independence.

a. Probability
b. Mean
c. Correlation
d. Frequency distribution

25. _________s are used in open sentences. For instance, in the formula x + 1 = 5, x is a _________ which represents an 'unknown' number. _________s are often represented by letters of the Roman alphabet, or those of other alphabets, such as Greek, and use other special symbols.
a. Quantitative
b. Personalization
c. Book of business
d. Variable

26. _________ is the process of measuring either the point of gaze ('where we are looking') or the motion of an eye relative to the head. An eye tracker is a device for measuring eye positions and eye movements. Eye trackers are used in research on the visual system, in psychology, in cognitive linguistics and in product design.
a. ADTECH
b. Eye tracking
c. ACNielsen
d. AMAX

27. _________ are used to collect quantitative information about items in a population. Surveys of human populations and institutions are common in political polling and government, health, social science and marketing research. A survey may focus on opinions or factual information depending on its purpose, and many surveys involve administering questions to individuals.
a. BeyondROI
b. Gross Margin Return on Inventory Investment
c. Statistical surveys
d. Convergent

28. A _________ is a tool used to measure the viewing habits of TV and cable audiences.

The _________ is a 'box', about the size of a paperback book. The box is hooked up to each television set and is accompanied by a remote control unit.

a. Power III
b. People Meter
c. 180SearchAssistant
d. 6-3-5 Brainwriting

29. _________ or _________ data refers to selected population characteristics as used in government, marketing or opinion research, or the _________ profiles used in such research. Note the distinction from the term 'demography' Commonly-used _________ include race, age, income, disabilities, mobility (in terms of travel time to work or number of vehicles available), educational attainment, home ownership, employment status, and even location.
a. AStore
b. African Americans
c. Albert Einstein
d. Demographic

30. _________ or Mystery Consumer is a tool used by market research companies to measure quality of retail service or gather specific information about products and services. Mystery shoppers posing as normal customers perform specific tasks--such as purchasing a product, asking questions, registering complaints or behaving in a certain way - and then provide detailed reports or feedback about their experiences.

_________ began in the 1940s as a way to measure employee integrity.

a. Market research
b. Mystery shopping
c. Questionnaire
d. Mystery shoppers

31. _________ is the examining of goods or services from retailers with the intent to purchase at that time. _________ is an activity of selection and/or purchase. In some contexts it is considered a leisure activity as well as an economic one.
a. Discount store
b. Hawkers
c. Khodebshchik
d. Shopping

1. _________ is defined by the American _________ Association as the activity, set of institutions, and processes for creating, communicating, delivering, and exchanging offerings that have value for customers, clients, partners, and society at large. The term developed from the original meaning which referred literally to going to market, as in shopping, or going to a market to sell goods or services.

_________ practice tends to be seen as a creative industry, which includes advertising, distribution and selling.

a. Marketing myopia
b. Product naming
c. Customer acquisition management
d. Marketing

2. _________ describes data and characteristics about the population or phenomenon being studied. _________ answers the questions who, what, where, when and how.

Although the data description is factual, accurate and systematic, the research cannot describe what caused a situation.

a. Two-tailed test
b. Sampling error
c. Power III
d. Descriptive research

3. _________ a research method involving the use of questionnaires and/or statistical surveys to gather data about people and their thoughts and behaviours.
a. Survey research
b. Z-test
c. Control chart
d. T-test

4. A number of different _________s are indicated below.

- Randomized controlled trial
  - Double-blind randomized trial
  - Single-blind randomized trial
  - Non-blind trial
- Nonrandomized trial (quasi-experiment)
  - Interrupted time series design (measures on a sample or a series of samples from the same population are obtained several times before and after a manipulated event or a naturally occurring event) - considered a type of quasi-experiment
- Cohort study
  - Prospective cohort
  - Retrospective cohort
  - Time series study
- Case-control study
  - Nested case-control study
- Cross-sectional study
  - Community survey (a type of cross-sectional study)

When choosing a _________, many factors must be taken into account. Different types of studies are subject to different types of bias. For example, recall bias is likely to occur in cross-sectional or case-control studies where subjects are asked to recall exposure to risk factors.

a. Longitudinal studies
b. Study design
c. Power III
d. 180SearchAssistant

5. A _________ attribute is one that exists in a range of magnitudes, and can therefore be measured. Measurements of any particular _________ property are expressed as a specific quantity, referred to as a unit, multiplied by a number. Examples of physical quantities are distance, mass, and time.
a. Dolly Dimples
b. BeyondROI
c. Quantitative
d. Lifestyle city

6. _________ is that part of statistical practice concerned with the selection of individual observations intended to yield some knowledge about a population of concern, especially for the purposes of statistical inference. Each observation measures one or more properties (weight, location, etc.) of an observable entity enumerated to distinguish objects or individuals.

a. Richard Buckminster 'Bucky' Fuller
b. Sports Marketing Group
c. AStore
d. Sampling

7. In statistics, _________ or estimation error is the error caused by observing a sample instead of the whole population.

An estimate of a quantity of interest, such as an average or percentage, will generally be subject to sample-to-sample variation. These variations in the possible sample values of a statistic can theoretically be expressed as _________s, although in practice the exact _________ is typically unknown.

a. Varimax rotation
b. Power III
c. Two-tailed test
d. Sampling error

8. _________ refer to a collection of facts usually collected as the result of experience, observation or experiment or a set of premises. This may consist of numbers, words particularly as measurements or observations of a set of variables. _________ are often viewed as a lowest level of abstraction from which information and knowledge are derived.

a. Mean
b. Sample size
c. Pearson product-moment correlation coefficient
d. Data

9. _________ is a process of gathering, modeling, and transforming data with the goal of highlighting useful information, suggesting conclusions, and supporting decision making. _________ has multiple facets and approaches, encompassing diverse techniques under a variety of names, in different business, science, and social science domains.

Data mining is a particular _________ technique that focuses on modeling and knowledge discovery for predictive rather than purely descriptive purposes.

a. 180SearchAssistant
b. Power III
c. 6-3-5 Brainwriting
d. Data analysis

10. In economics, business, retail, and accounting, a _________ is the value of money that has been used up to produce something, and hence is not available for use anymore. In economics, a _________ is an alternative that is given up as a result of a decision. In business, the _________ may be one of acquisition, in which case the amount of money expended to acquire it is counted as _________.

a. Transaction cost
b. Fixed costs
c. Variable cost
d. Cost

11. Advertising mail junk mail is the delivery of advertising material to recipients of postal mail. The delivery of advertising mail forms a large and growing service for many postal services, and _________ marketing forms a significant portion of the direct marketing industry. Some organizations attempt to help people opt-out of receiving advertising mail, in many cases motivated by a concern over its negative environmental impact.

a. Directory Harvest Attack
b. Phishing
c. Telemarketing
d. Direct mail

12. _________ are used to collect quantitative information about items in a population. Surveys of human populations and institutions are common in political polling and government, health, social science and marketing research. A survey may focus on opinions or factual information depending on its purpose, and many surveys involve administering questions to individuals.

a. Gross Margin Return on Inventory Investment
b. Statistical surveys
c. BeyondROI
d. Convergent

13. _________ is a standard point of view or personal prejudice. especially when the tendency interferes with the ability to be impartial, unprejudiced, or objective. The term _________ed is used to describe an action, judgment, or other outcome influenced by a prejudged perspective.

a. Power III
b. Bias
c. 180SearchAssistant
d. 6-3-5 Brainwriting

14. _________ generally refers to a list of all planned expenses and revenues. It is a plan for saving and spending. A _________ is an important concept in microeconomics, which uses a _________ line to illustrate the trade-offs between two or more goods.

a. 6-3-5 Brainwriting
b. 180SearchAssistant
c. Power III
d. Budget

15. In economics and sociology, an _________ is any factor (financial or non-financial) that enables or motivates a particular course of action, or counts as a reason for preferring one choice to the alternatives. It is an expectation that encourages people to behave in a certain way. Since human beings are purposeful creatures, the study of _________ structures is central to the study of all economic activity (both in terms of individual decision-making and in terms of co-operation and competition within a larger institutional structure.)
a. ADTECH
b. AMAX
c. ACNielsen
d. Incentive

16. A _________, in the field of business and marketing, is a geographic region or demographic group used to gauge the viability of a product or service in the mass market prior to a wide scale roll-out. The criteria used to judge the acceptability of a _________ region or group include:

1. a population that is demographically similar to the proposed target market; and
2. relative isolation from densely populated media markets so that advertising to the test audience can be efficient and economical.

The _________ ideally aims to duplicate 'everything' - promotion and distribution as well as `product' - on a smaller scale. The technique replicates, typically in one area, what is planned to occur in a national launch; and the results are very carefully monitored, so that they can be extrapolated to projected national results. The `area' may be any one of the following:

- Television area
- Test town
- Residential neighborhood
- Test site

A number of decisions have to be taken about any _________:

- Which _________?
- What is to be tested?
- How long a test?
- What are the success criteria?

The simple go or no-go decision, together with the related reduction of risk, is normally the main justification for the expense of _________s. At the same time, however, such _________s can be used to test specific elements of a new product's marketing mix; possibly the version of the product itself, the promotional message and media spend, the distribution channels and the price.

a. 180SearchAssistant
b. Power III
c. Test market
d. Preadolescence

17. _________s are used in open sentences. For instance, in the formula x + 1 = 5, x is a _________ which represents an 'unknown' number. _________s are often represented by letters of the Roman alphabet, or those of other alphabets, such as Greek, and use other special symbols.

a. Book of business
b. Variable
c. Personalization
d. Quantitative

18. The terms '_________' and 'independent variable' are used in similar but subtly different ways in mathematics and statistics as part of the standard terminology in those subjects. They are used to distinguish between two types of quantities being considered, separating them into those available at the start of a process and those being created by it, where the latter (_________s) are dependent on the former (independent variables.)

In traditional calculus, a function is defined as a relation between two terms called variables because their values vary.

a. Power III
b. 180SearchAssistant
c. Field experiment
d. Dependent variable

19. In economics, an externality or spillover of an economic transaction is an impact on a party that is not directly involved in the transaction. In such a case, prices do not reflect the full costs or benefits in production or consumption of a product or service. A positive impact is called an _________ benefit, while a negative impact is called an _________ cost.

a. ADTECH
b. AMAX
c. ACNielsen
d. External

20. _________ is the validity of generalized (causal) inferences in scientific studies, usually based on experiments as experimental validity.

Inferences about cause-effect relationships based on a specific scientific study are said to possess _________ if they may be generalized from the unique and idiosyncratic settings, procedures and participants to other populations and conditions Causal inferences said to possess high degrees of _________ can reasonably be expected to apply (a) to the target population of the study (i.e. from which the sample was drawn) (also referred to as population validity), and (b) to the universe of other populations (e.g. across time and space.)

The most common loss of _________ comes from the fact that experiments using human participants often employ small samples obtained from a single geographic location or with idiosyncratic features (e.g. volunteers.)

a. ADTECH
b. AMAX
c. External validity
d. ACNielsen

21. _________ is the validity of (causal) inferences in scientific studies, usually based on experiments as experimental validity .

Inferences are said to possess _________ if a causal relation between two variables is properly demonstrated . A causal inference may be based on a relation when three criteria are satisfied:

1. the 'cause' precedes the 'effect' in time (temporal precedence),
2. the 'cause' and the 'effect' are related (covariation), and
3. there are no plausible alternative explanations for the observed covariation (nonspuriousness) .

In scientific experimental settings, researchers often manipulate a variable (the independent variable) to see what effect it has on a second variable (the dependent variable) For example, a researcher might, for different experimental groups, manipulate the dosage of a particular drug between groups to see what effect it has on health. In this example, the researcher wants to make a causal inference, namely, that different doses of the drug may be held responsible for observed changes or differences.

a. AMAX
b. ADTECH
c. ACNielsen
d. Internal validity

22. _________ are variables other than the independent variable that may bear any effect on the behavior of the subject being studied.

_________ are often classified into three main types:

1. Subject variables, which are the characteristics of the individuals being studied that might affect their actions. These variables include age, gender, health status, mood, background, etc.
2. Experimental variables are characteristics of the persons conducting the experiment which might influence how a person behaves. Gender, the presence of racial discrimination, language, or other factors may qualify as such variables.
3. Situational variables are features of the environment in which the study or research was conducted, which have a bearing on the outcome of the experiment in a negative way. Included are the air temperature, level of activity, lighting, and the time of day.

There are two strategies of controlling _________. Either a potentially influential variable is kept the same for all subjects in the research, or they balance the variables in a group.

Take for example an experiment, in which a salesperson sells clothing on a door-to-door basis.

a. Extraneous variables
b. AMAX
c. ADTECH
d. ACNielsen

23. A _________ applies the scientific method to experimentally examine an intervention in the real world (or as many experimental economists like to say, naturally-occurring environments) rather than in the laboratory. _________s, like lab experiments, generally randomize subjects (or other sampling units) into treatment and control groups and compare outcomes between these groups. Clinical trials of pharmaceuticals are one example of _________s.
a. 180SearchAssistant
b. Response variable
c. Field experiment
d. Power III

24. Competitiveness is a comparative concept of the ability and performance of a firm, sub-sector or country to sell and supply goods and/or services in a given market. Although widely used in economics and business management, the usefulness of the concept, particularly in the context of national competitiveness, is vigorously disputed by economists, such as Paul Krugman .

The term may also be applied to markets, where it is used to refer to the extent to which the market structure may be regarded as perfectly _________.

a. Geographical pricing
b. Free trade zone
c. Customs union
d. Competitive

25. A _________ is a structured collection of records or data that is stored in a computer system. The structure is achieved by organizing the data according to a _________ model. The model in most common use today is the relational model.

a. 6-3-5 Brainwriting
b. Database
c. Power III
d. 180SearchAssistant

1. _________ is an independent technology and market research company that provides its clients with advice about technology's impact on business and consumers. _________ has four research centers in the US: Cambridge, Massachusetts; Foster City, California; Washington, D.C.; and Westport, Connecticut. It also has four European research centers in Amsterdam, Frankfurt, London, and Paris.

a. Mapinfo
b. BigMachines
c. GlobalSpec
d. Forrester Research

2. _________ is that part of statistical practice concerned with the selection of individual observations intended to yield some knowledge about a population of concern, especially for the purposes of statistical inference. Each observation measures one or more properties (weight, location, etc.) of an observable entity enumerated to distinguish objects or individuals.

a. AStore
b. Richard Buckminster 'Bucky' Fuller
c. Sports Marketing Group
d. Sampling

3. _________ is a form of Internet marketing that seeks to promote websites by increasing their visibility in search engine result pages (SERPs.) According to the _________ Professional Organization, _________ methods include: search engine optimization (or SEO), paid placement, contextual advertising, and paid inclusion. Other sources, including the New York Times, define _________ as the practice of buying paid search listings.

a. Search engine marketing
b. Pay for placement
c. Display advertising
d. Blog marketing

4. _________ is defined by the American _________ Association as the activity, set of institutions, and processes for creating, communicating, delivering, and exchanging offerings that have value for customers, clients, partners, and society at large. The term developed from the original meaning which referred literally to going to market, as in shopping, or going to a market to sell goods or services.

_________ practice tends to be seen as a creative industry, which includes advertising, distribution and selling.

a. Customer acquisition management
b. Marketing myopia
c. Product naming
d. Marketing

5. The United States _________ is the government agency that is responsible for the United States Census. It also gathers other national demographic and economic data.

a. Census Bureau
b. 180SearchAssistant
c. Power III
d. 6-3-5 Brainwriting

6. A _________ is a research instrument consisting of a series of questions and other prompts for the purpose of gathering information from respondents. Although they are often designed for statistical analysis of the responses, this is not always the case. The _________ was invented by Sir Francis Galton.

a. Mystery shoppers
b. Mystery shopping
c. Questionnaire
d. Market research

7. _________ is a standard point of view or personal prejudice. especially when the tendency interferes with the ability to be impartial, unprejudiced, or objective. The term _________ed is used to describe an action, judgment, or other outcome influenced by a prejudged perspective.

a. Bias
b. 6-3-5 Brainwriting
c. 180SearchAssistant
d. Power III

8. The _________ of a statistical sample is the number of observations that constitute it. It is typically denoted n, a positive integer (natural number.)

Typically, all else being equal, a larger _________ leads to increased precision in estimates of various properties of the population.

a. Frequency distribution
b. Heteroskedastic
c. Data
d. Sample size

9. In statistics, _________ or estimation error is the error caused by observing a sample instead of the whole population.

An estimate of a quantity of interest, such as an average or percentage, will generally be subject to sample-to-sample variation. These variations in the possible sample values of a statistic can theoretically be expressed as _________s, although in practice the exact _________ is typically unknown.

a. Sampling error
b. Two-tailed test
c. Varimax rotation
d. Power III

10. _________ refer to a collection of facts usually collected as the result of experience, observation or experiment or a set of premises. This may consist of numbers, words particularly as measurements or observations of a set of variables. _________ are often viewed as a lowest level of abstraction from which information and knowledge are derived.

a. Mean
b. Pearson product-moment correlation coefficient
c. Sample size
d. Data

11. _________ is a term used to describe a process of preparing and collecting data - for example as part of a process improvement or similar project.

_________ usually takes place early on in an improvement project, and is often formalised through a _________ Plan which often contains the following activity.

1. Pre collection activity - Agree goals, target data, definitions, methods
2. Collection - _________
3. Present Findings - usually involves some form of sorting analysis and/or presentation.

A formal _________ process is necessary as it ensures that data gathered is both defined and accurate and that subsequent decisions based on arguments embodied in the findings are valid . The process provides both a baseline from which to measure from and in certain cases a target on what to improve. Types of _________ 1-By mail questionnaires 2-By personal interview

- Six sigma
- Sampling (statistics)

.

a. 180SearchAssistant
b. Power III
c. 6-3-5 Brainwriting
d. Data collection

12. _________ is a way of expressing knowledge or belief that an event will occur or has occurred. In mathematics the concept has been given an exact meaning in _________ theory, that is used extensively in such areas of study as mathematics, statistics, finance, gambling, science, and philosophy to draw conclusions about the likelihood of potential events and the underlying mechanics of complex systems.
a. Linear regression
b. Data
c. Probability
d. Heteroskedastic

13. Sampling is the use of a subset of the population to represent the whole population. Probability sampling, or random sampling, is a sampling technique in which the probability of getting any particular sample may be calculated. _________ does not meet this criterion and should be used with caution.
a. Power III
b. Nonprobability sampling
c. Quota sampling
d. Snowball sampling

14. In statistics, a simple random sample is a subset of individuals (a sample) chosen from a larger set (a population.) Each individual is chosen randomly and entirely by chance, such that each individual has the same probability of being chosen at any stage during the sampling process, and each subset of k individuals has the same probability of being chosen for the sample as any other subset of k individuals (.) This process and technique is known as _________, and should not be confused with Random Sampling.
a. Market analysis
b. Logit analysis
c. Focus group
d. Simple random sampling

15. In statistics, the _________ is a common measure of the correlation (linear dependence) between two variables X and Y. It is very widely used in the sciences as a measure of the strength of linear dependence between two variables, giving a value somewhere between +1 and -1 inclusive. It was first introduced by Francis Galton in the 1880s, and named after Karl Pearson.

In accordance with the usual convention, when calculated for an entire population, the Pearson product-moment correlation is typically designated by the analogous Greek letter, which in this case is ρ .

a. Control chart
b. Standard deviation
c. Pearson product-moment correlation coefficient
d. Median

16. _________ is a sampling technique used when 'natural' groupings are evident in a statistical population. It is often used in marketing research. In this technique, the total population is divided into these groups (or clusters) and a sample of the groups is selected.
a. Power III
b. Quota sampling
c. Cluster sampling
d. Snowball sampling

17. In probability theory and statistics, _________ indicates the strength and direction of a linear relationship between two random variables. That is in contrast with the usage of the term in colloquial speech, denoting any relationship, not necessarily linear. In general statistical usage, _________ or co-relation refers to the departure of two random variables from independence.
a. Correlation
b. Probability
c. Mean
d. Frequency distribution

18. In statistics, _________ is a method of sampling from a population.

When sub-populations vary considerably, it is advantageous to sample each subpopulation (stratum) independently. Stratification is the process of grouping members of the population into relatively homogeneous subgroups before sampling.

a. T-test
b. Coefficient of variation
c. Stratified sampling
d. Data

19. _________ is anything that is intended to save time, energy or frustration. A _________ store at a petrol station, for example, sells items that have nothing to do with gasoline/petrol, but it saves the consumer from having to go to a grocery store. '_________' is a very relative term and its meaning tends to change over time.

a. Convenience
b. MaxDiff
c. Demographic profile
d. Marketing buzz

20. _________ is a type of nonprobability sampling which involves the sample being drawn from that part of the population which is close to hand. That is, a sample population selected because it is readily available and convenient. The researcher using such a sample cannot scientifically make generalizations about the total population from this sample because it would not be representative enough.

a. ADTECH
b. AMAX
c. ACNielsen
d. Accidental sampling

21. In the United States, the Office of Management and Budget (OMB) has produced a formal definition of metropolitan areas. These are referred to as '_________s' (_________s) and 'Combined Statistical Areas.' An earlier version of the _________ was the 'Standard _________' (SMetropolitan statistical area.) _________s are composed of counties and for some county equivalents.

a. Power III
b. Metropolitan statistical area
c. 180SearchAssistant
d. Race and ethnicity in the United States Census

22. In _________, the population is first segmented into mutually exclusive sub-groups, just as in stratified sampling. Then judgment is used to select the subjects or units from each segment based on a specified proportion. For example, an interviewer may be told to sample 200 females and 300 males between the age of 45 and 60.

a. Power III
b. Nonprobability sampling
c. Snowball sampling
d. Quota sampling

23. In social science research, _________ is a technique for developing a research sample where existing study subjects recruit future subjects from among their acquaintances. Thus the sample group appears to grow like a rolling snowball. As the sample builds up, enough data is gathered to be useful for research.

a. Quota sampling
b. Nonprobability sampling
c. Power III
d. Snowball sampling

24. In algebra, a _________ is a function depending on n that associates a scalar, det(A), to an n×n square matrix A. The fundamental geometric meaning of a _________ is a scale factor for measure when A is regarded as a linear transformation. _________s are important both in calculus, where they enter the substitution rule for several variables, and in multilinear algebra.

For a fixed nonnegative integer n, there is a unique _________ function for the n×n matrices over any commutative ring R. In particular, this function exists when R is the field of real or complex numbers.

a. Motion Picture Association of America's film-rating system
b. Package-on-Package
c. Black Friday
d. Determinant

25. Human beings are also considered to be _________ because they have the ability to change raw materials into valuable _________. The term Human _________ can also be defined as the skills, energies, talents, abilities and knowledge that are used for the production of goods or the rendering of services. While taking into account human beings as _________, the following things have to be kept in mind:

- The size of the population
- The capabilities of the individuals in that population

Many _________ cannot be consumed in their original form. They have to be processed in order to change them into more usable commodities.

a. 6-3-5 Brainwriting
b. Resources
c. Power III
d. 180SearchAssistant

26. _________ is a term commonly used to describe commerce transactions between businesses like the one between a manufacturer and a wholesaler or a wholesaler and a retailer i.e both the buyer and the seller are business entity.This is unlike business-to-consumers (B2C) which involve a business entity and end consumer, or business-to-government (B2G) which involve a business entity and government.

The volume of B2B transactions is much higher than the volume of B2C transactions. The primary reason for this is that in a typical supply chain there will be many B2B transactions involving subcomponent or raw materials, and only one B2C transaction, specifically sale of the finished product to the end customer.

a. Social marketing
b. Business-to-business
c. Customer relationship management
d. Disruptive technology

27. A sample is a subject chosen from a population for investigation. A _________ is one chosen by a method involving an unpredictable component. Random sampling can also refer to taking a number of independent observations from the same probability distribution, without involving any real population.

a. Random sample
b. Selection bias
c. 180SearchAssistant
d. Power III

1. _________, a business term, is a measure of how products and services supplied by a company meet or surpass customer expectation. It is seen as a key performance indicator within business and is part of the four perspectives of a Balanced Scorecard.

In a competitive marketplace where businesses compete for customers, _________ is seen as a key differentiator and increasingly has become a key element of business strategy.

a. Psychological pricing
b. Customer base
c. Supplier diversity
d. Customer Satisfaction

2. A personal and cultural _________ is a relative ethic _________, an assumption upon which implementation can be extrapolated. A _________ system is a set of consistent _________s and measures that is soo not true. A principle _________ is a foundation upon which other _________s and measures of integrity are based.
a. Value
b. Supreme Court of the United States
c. Perceptual maps
d. Package-on-Package

3. In environmental modeling and especially in hydrology, a _________ model means a model that is acceptably consistent with observed natural processes, i.e. that simulates well, for example, observed river discharge. It is a key concept of the so-called Generalized Likelihood Uncertainty Estimation (GLUE) methodology to quantify how uncertain environmental predictions are.
a. 180SearchAssistant
b. Power III
c. 6-3-5 Brainwriting
d. Behavioral

4. _________s are used in open sentences. For instance, in the formula x + 1 = 5, x is a _________ which represents an 'unknown' number. _________s are often represented by letters of the Roman alphabet, or those of other alphabets, such as Greek, and use other special symbols.
a. Personalization
b. Quantitative
c. Book of business
d. Variable

5. A _________ is a collection of symbols, experiences and associations connected with a product, a service, a person or any other artifact or entity.

_________s have become increasingly important components of culture and the economy, now being described as 'cultural accessories and personal philosophies'.

Some people distinguish the psychological aspect of a _________ from the experiential aspect.

a. Brandable software
b. Brand equity
c. Store brand
d. Brand

6. _________, in marketing, consists of a consumer's commitment to repurchase the brand and can be demonstrated by repeated buying of a product or service or other positive behaviors such as word of mouth advocacy. True _________ implies that the consumer is willing, at least on occasion, to put aside their own desires in the interest of the brand. _________ has been proclaimed by some to be the ultimate goal of marketing.

a. Trade Symbols
b. Brand implementation
c. Brand awareness
d. Brand loyalty

7. _________ is an advertisement in which a particular product specifically mentions a competitor by name for the express purpose of showing why the competitor is inferior to the product naming it.

This should not be confused with parody advertisements, where a fictional product is being advertised for the purpose of poking fun at the particular advertisement, nor should it be confused with the use of a coined brand name for the purpose of comparing the product without actually naming an actual competitor. ('Wikipedia tastes better and is less filling than the Encyclopedia Galactica.')

In the 1980s, during what has been referred to as the cola wars, soft-drink manufacturer Pepsi ran a series of advertisements where people, caught on hidden camera, in a blind taste test, chose Pepsi over rival Coca-Cola.

a. Cost per conversion
b. GL-70
c. Comparative advertising
d. Heavy-up

8. _________ are used to collect quantitative information about items in a population. Surveys of human populations and institutions are common in political polling and government, health, social science and marketing research. A survey may focus on opinions or factual information depending on its purpose, and many surveys involve administering questions to individuals.

a. BeyondROI
b. Statistical surveys
c. Convergent
d. Gross Margin Return on Inventory Investment

9. _________ refer to a collection of facts usually collected as the result of experience, observation or experiment or a set of premises. This may consist of numbers, words particularly as measurements or observations of a set of variables. _________ are often viewed as a lowest level of abstraction from which information and knowledge are derived.

a. Sample size
b. Mean
c. Pearson product-moment correlation coefficient
d. Data

10. _________ is a property of a test intended to measure something. The test is said to have _________ if it 'looks like' it is going to measure what it is supposed to measure. For instance, if you prepare a test to measure whether students can perform multiplication, and the people you show it to all agree that it looks like a good test of multiplication ability, you have shown the _________ of your test.

a. 180SearchAssistant
b. Power III
c. Face validity
d. Selective distortion

11. In statistics, analysis of variance (_________) is a collection of statistical models, and their associated procedures, in which the observed variance is partitioned into components due to different explanatory variables. In its simplest form _________ gives a statistical test of whether the means of several groups are all equal, and therefore generalizes Student's two-sample t-test to more than two groups.

There are three conceptual classes of such models:

1. Fixed-effects models assumes that the data came from normal populations which may differ only in their means. (Model 1)
2. Random effects models assume that the data describe a hierarchy of different populations whose differences are constrained by the hierarchy. (Model 2)
3. Mixed-effect models describe situations where both fixed and random effects are present. (Model 3)

In practice, there are several types of _________ depending on the number of treatments and the way they are applied to the subjects in the experiment:

- One-way _________ is used to test for differences among two or more independent groups. Typically, however, the one-way _________ is used to test for differences among at least three groups, since the two-group case can be covered by a T-test (Gossett, 1908.)

a. AMAX
b. ADTECH
c. ACNielsen
d. ANOVA

12. In statistics, a _________ is a tabulation of the values that one or more variables take in a sample.

Univariate _________s are often presented as lists, ordered by quantity, showing the number of times each value appears. For example, if 100 people rate a five-point Likert scale assessing their agreement with a statement on a scale on which 1 denotes strong agreement and 5 strong disagreement, the _________ of their responses might look like:

This simple tabulation has two drawbacks.

a. Statistics
b. Frequency distribution
c. Survey research
d. Confidence interval

13. In statistics, _________ has two related meanings:

- the arithmetic _________
- the expected value of a random variable, which is also called the population _________.

It is sometimes stated that the '_________' _________s average. This is incorrect if '_________' is taken in the specific sense of 'arithmetic _________' as there are different types of averages: the _________, median, and mode. For instance, average house prices almost always use the median value for the average. These three types of averages are all measures of locations.

a. Confidence interval
b. Standard normal distribution
c. Heteroskedastic
d. Mean

14. In probability theory and statistics, a _________ is described as the number separating the higher half of a sample, a population from the lower half. The _________ of a finite list of numbers can be found by arranging all the observations from lowest value to highest value and picking the middle one. If there is an even number of observations, the _________ is not unique, so one often takes the mean of the two middle values.
a. Frequency distribution
b. Statistically significant
c. Linear regression
d. Median

15. In descriptive statistics, the _________ is the length of the smallest interval which contains all the data. It is calculated by subtracting the smallest observation (sample minimum) from the greatest (sample maximum) and provides an indication of statistical dispersion.

It is measured in the same units as the data.

a. Range
b. Personalization
c. Just-In-Case
d. Japan Advertising Photographers' Association

16. _________ is a computer program used for statistical analysis.

_________ (originally, Statistical Package for the Social Sciences) was released in its first version in 1968 after being founded by Norman Nie and C. Hadlai Hull. Nie was then a political science postgraduate at Stanford University,and now Research Professor in the Department of Political Science at Stanford and Professor Emeritus of Political Science at the University of Chicago.

a. 180SearchAssistant
b. Power III
c. 6-3-5 Brainwriting
d. SPSS

17. In statistics, _________ is a simple measure of the variability or dispersion of a data set. A low _________ indicates that the data points tend to be very close to the same value (the mean), while high _________ indicates that the data are 'spread out' over a large range of values.

For example, the average height for adult men in the United States is about 70 inches, with a _________ of around 3 inches.

a. Statistically significant
b. Standard deviation
c. Z-test
d. Pearson product-moment correlation coefficient

18. _________ is one of the four elements of marketing mix. An organization or set of organizations (go-betweens) involved in the process of making a product or service available for use or consumption by a consumer or business user.

The other three parts of the marketing mix are product, pricing, and promotion.

a. Comparison-Shopping agent
b. Better Living Through Chemistry
c. Japan Advertising Photographers' Association
d. Distribution

19. The '_________' is an expression which typically refers to the theory of scale types developed by the Harvard psychologist Stanley Smith Stevens In this article Stevens claimed that all measurement in science was conducted using four different types of numerical scales which he called 'nominal', 'ordinal', 'interval' and 'ratio'.

a. Power III
b. 180SearchAssistant
c. 6-3-5 Brainwriting
d. Levels of measurement

20. A _________ is a psychometric scale commonly used in questionnaires, and is the most widely used scale in survey research. When responding to a Likert questionnaire item, respondents specify their level of agreement to a statement. The scale is named after its inventor, psychologist Rensis Likert.

a. Factor analysis
b. Semantic differential
c. Likert scale
d. Power III

21. _________ is a type of a rating scale designed to measure the connotative meaning of objects, events, and concepts. The connotations are used to derive the attitude towards the given object, event or concept.

Osgood's _________ was designed to measure the connotative meaning of concepts.

a. Factor analysis
b. Likert scale
c. Power III
d. Semantic differential

22. The term _________, invented to replace the older gender-based terms, is a typical example of a gender-neutral neologism.

In the present media-sensitive world, many organizations are increasingly likely to employ professionals who have received formal training in journalism, communications, public relations and public affairs in this role in order to ensure that public announcements are made in the most appropriate fashion and through the most appropriate channels to maximize the impact of favorable messages, and to minimize the impact of unfavorable messages. Popular local and national sports stars are often chosen as spokespeople for commercial advertising.

a. 180SearchAssistant
b. Power III
c. Professional services
d. Spokesperson

23. In grammar, the _________ is the form of an adjective or adverb which denotes the degree or grade by which a person, thing and is used in this context with a subordinating conjunction, such as than, as...as, etc.

The structure of a _________ in English consists normally of the positive form of the adjective or adverb, plus the suffix -er e.g. 'he is taller than his father is', or 'the village is less picturesque than the town nearby'.

a. Power III
b. Comparative
c. 6-3-5 Brainwriting
d. 180SearchAssistant

24. The loyalty business model is a business model used in strategic management in which company resources are employed so as to increase the loyalty of customers and other stakeholders in the expectation that corporate objectives will be met or surpassed. A typical example of this type of model is: quality of product or service leads to customer satisfaction, which leads to _________, which leads to profitability.

Fredrick Reichheld (1996) expanded the loyalty business model beyond customers and employees.

a. 180SearchAssistant
b. 6-3-5 Brainwriting
c. Power III
d. Customer loyalty

1. A _________ is a research instrument consisting of a series of questions and other prompts for the purpose of gathering information from respondents. Although they are often designed for statistical analysis of the responses, this is not always the case. The _________ was invented by Sir Francis Galton.
   a. Market research
   b. Mystery shopping
   c. Questionnaire
   d. Mystery shoppers

2. _________ describes data and characteristics about the population or phenomenon being studied. _________ answers the questions who, what, where, when and how.

Although the data description is factual, accurate and systematic, the research cannot describe what caused a situation.

   a. Power III
   b. Sampling error
   c. Two-tailed test
   d. Descriptive research

3. _________ a research method involving the use of questionnaires and/or statistical surveys to gather data about people and their thoughts and behaviours.
   a. Z-test
   b. Survey research
   c. Control chart
   d. T-test

4. A _________ is a statement or claim that a particular event will occur in the future in more certain terms than a forecast. The etymology of this word is Latin . In regards to predicting the future Howard H. Stevenson Says, ' _________ is at least two things: Important and hard.' Important, because we have to act, and hard because we have to realize the future we want, and what is the best way to get there.
   a. 180SearchAssistant
   b. Prediction
   c. Power III
   d. 6-3-5 Brainwriting

5. A number of different _________s are indicated below.

- Randomized controlled trial
  - Double-blind randomized trial
  - Single-blind randomized trial
  - Non-blind trial
- Nonrandomized trial (quasi-experiment)
  - Interrupted time series design (measures on a sample or a series of samples from the same population are obtained several times before and after a manipulated event or a naturally occurring event) - considered a type of quasi-experiment

- Cohort study
  - Prospective cohort
  - Retrospective cohort
  - Time series study
- Case-control study
  - Nested case-control study
- Cross-sectional study
  - Community survey (a type of cross-sectional study)

When choosing a _________, many factors must be taken into account. Different types of studies are subject to different types of bias. For example, recall bias is likely to occur in cross-sectional or case-control studies where subjects are asked to recall exposure to risk factors.

a. Longitudinal studies
b. 180SearchAssistant
c. Power III
d. Study design

6. A personal and cultural _________ is a relative ethic _________, an assumption upon which implementation can be extrapolated. A _________ system is a set of consistent _________s and measures that is soo not true. A principle _________ is a foundation upon which other _________s and measures of integrity are based.

a. Supreme Court of the United States
b. Value
c. Perceptual maps
d. Package-on-Package

7. _________ refer to a collection of facts usually collected as the result of experience, observation or experiment or a set of premises. This may consist of numbers, words particularly as measurements or observations of a set of variables. _________ are often viewed as a lowest level of abstraction from which information and knowledge are derived.

a. Sample size
b. Mean
c. Pearson product-moment correlation coefficient
d. Data

8. _________ is a term used to describe a process of preparing and collecting data - for example as part of a process improvement or similar project.

_________ usually takes place early on in an improvement project, and is often formalised through a _________ Plan which often contains the following activity.

1. Pre collection activity - Agree goals, target data, definitions, methods
2. Collection - _________
3. Present Findings - usually involves some form of sorting analysis and/or presentation.

A formal _________ process is necessary as it ensures that data gathered is both defined and accurate and that subsequent decisions based on arguments embodied in the findings are valid . The process provides both a baseline from which to measure from and in certain cases a target on what to improve. Types of _________ 1-By mail questionnaires 2-By personal interview

- Six sigma
- Sampling (statistics)

.

a. 180SearchAssistant
b. 6-3-5 Brainwriting
c. Power III
d. Data collection

9. _________ or _________ data refers to selected population characteristics as used in government, marketing or opinion research, or the _________ profiles used in such research. Note the distinction from the term 'demography' Commonly-used _________ include race, age, income, disabilities, mobility (in terms of travel time to work or number of vehicles available), educational attainment, home ownership, employment status, and even location.
a. African Americans
b. Albert Einstein
c. AStore
d. Demographic

10. In statistics, the _________ is a common measure of the correlation (linear dependence) between two variables X and Y. It is very widely used in the sciences as a measure of the strength of linear dependence between two variables, giving a value somewhere between +1 and -1 inclusive. It was first introduced by Francis Galton in the 1880s, and named after Karl Pearson.

In accordance with the usual convention, when calculated for an entire population, the Pearson product-moment correlation is typically designated by the analogous Greek letter, which in this case is ρ .

a. Pearson product-moment correlation coefficient
b. Control chart
c. Standard deviation
d. Median

11. In probability theory and statistics, _________ indicates the strength and direction of a linear relationship between two random variables. That is in contrast with the usage of the term in colloquial speech, denoting any relationship, not necessarily linear. In general statistical usage, _________ or co-relation refers to the departure of two random variables from independence.

a. Probability
b. Correlation
c. Mean
d. Frequency distribution

1. _________ refer to a collection of facts usually collected as the result of experience, observation or experiment or a set of premises. This may consist of numbers, words particularly as measurements or observations of a set of variables. _________ are often viewed as a lowest level of abstraction from which information and knowledge are derived.

a. Data
b. Mean
c. Sample size
d. Pearson product-moment correlation coefficient

2. _________ is a process of gathering, modeling, and transforming data with the goal of highlighting useful information, suggesting conclusions, and supporting decision making. _________ has multiple facets and approaches, encompassing diverse techniques under a variety of names, in different business, science, and social science domains.

Data mining is a particular _________ technique that focuses on modeling and knowledge discovery for predictive rather than purely descriptive purposes.

a. Power III
b. 6-3-5 Brainwriting
c. 180SearchAssistant
d. Data analysis

3. A _________ attribute is one that exists in a range of magnitudes, and can therefore be measured. Measurements of any particular _________ property are expressed as a specific quantity, referred to as a unit, multiplied by a number. Examples of physical quantities are distance, mass, and time.

a. Lifestyle city
b. Dolly Dimples
c. Quantitative
d. BeyondROI

4. _________ is a term used to describe a process of preparing and collecting data - for example as part of a process improvement or similar project.

_________ usually takes place early on in an improvement project, and is often formalised through a _________ Plan which often contains the following activity.

1. Pre collection activity - Agree goals, target data, definitions, methods
2. Collection - _________
3. Present Findings - usually involves some form of sorting analysis and/or presentation.

A formal _________ process is necessary as it ensures that data gathered is both defined and accurate and that subsequent decisions based on arguments embodied in the findings are valid . The process provides both a baseline from which to measure from and in certain cases a target on what to improve. Types of _________ 1-By mail questionnaires 2-By personal interview

- Six sigma
- Sampling (statistics)

.

a. Power III
b. 6-3-5 Brainwriting
c. Data collection
d. 180SearchAssistant

5. A _________ is a form of qualitative research in which a group of people are asked about their attitude towards a product, service, concept, advertisement, idea, or packaging. Questions are asked in an interactive group setting where participants are free to talk with other group members.

Ernest Dichter originated the idea of having a 'group therapy' for products and this process is what became known as a _________.

a. Marketing research process
b. Logit analysis
c. Cross tabulation
d. Focus group

6. An _________ is one type of focus group, and is a sub-set of online research methods.

A moderator invites prescreened, qualified respondents who represent the target of interest to log on to conferencing software at a pre-arranged time and to take part in an _________. Some researchers will offer incentives for participating but this raises a number of ethical questions.

a. Intangibility
b. Automated surveys
c. Engagement
d. Online focus group

7. _________ is a genre of writing that uses fieldwork to provide a descriptive study of human societies. _________ presents the results of a holistic research method founded on the idea that a system's properties cannot necessarily be accurately understood independently of each other. The genre has both formal and historical connections to travel writing and colonial office reports.

a. ADTECH
b. Ethnography
c. AMAX
d. ACNielsen

8. _________ is a field of inquiry that crosscuts disciplines and subject matters . _________ers aim to gather an in-depth understanding of human behavior and the reasons that govern such behavior. The discipline investigates the why and how of decision making, not just what, where, when.

a. 180SearchAssistant
b. 6-3-5 Brainwriting
c. Power III
d. Qualitative research

9. _________ is the examining of goods or services from retailers with the intent to purchase at that time. _________ is an activity of selection and/or purchase. In some contexts it is considered a leisure activity as well as an economic one.

a. Khodebshchik
b. Discount store
c. Shopping
d. Hawkers

10. _________ is a form of communication that typically attempts to persuade potential customers to purchase or to consume more of a particular brand of product or service. 'While now central to the contemporary global economy and the reproduction of global production networks, it is only quite recently that _________ has been more than a marginal influence on patterns of sales and production. The formation of modern _________ was intimately bound up with the emergence of new forms of monopoly capitalism around the end of the 19th and beginning of the 20th century as one element in corporate strategies to create, organize and where possible control markets, especially for mass produced consumer goods.

a. AMAX
b. ADTECH
c. Advertising
d. ACNielsen

11. In statistics, the _________ is a common measure of the correlation (linear dependence) between two variables X and Y. It is very widely used in the sciences as a measure of the strength of linear dependence between two variables, giving a value somewhere between +1 and -1 inclusive. It was first introduced by Francis Galton in the 1880s, and named after Karl Pearson.

In accordance with the usual convention, when calculated for an entire population, the Pearson product-moment correlation is typically designated by the analogous Greek letter, which in this case is ρ .

a. Control chart
b. Standard deviation
c. Pearson product-moment correlation coefficient
d. Median

12. In probability theory and statistics, _________ indicates the strength and direction of a linear relationship between two random variables. That is in contrast with the usage of the term in colloquial speech, denoting any relationship, not necessarily linear. In general statistical usage, _________ or co-relation refers to the departure of two random variables from independence.

a. Mean
b. Frequency distribution
c. Correlation
d. Probability

13. _________ is a concept that denotes the precise probability of specific eventualities. Technically, the notion of _________ is independent from the notion of value and, as such, eventualities may have both beneficial and adverse consequences. However, in general usage the convention is to focus only on potential negative impact to some characteristic of value that may arise from a future event.

a. Power III
b. 6-3-5 Brainwriting
c. 180SearchAssistant
d. Risk

14. A _________ is a research instrument consisting of a series of questions and other prompts for the purpose of gathering information from respondents. Although they are often designed for statistical analysis of the responses, this is not always the case. The _________ was invented by Sir Francis Galton.

a. Market research
b. Questionnaire
c. Mystery shoppers
d. Mystery shopping

15. _________ is a term used in business for a short document that summarises a longer report, proposal or group of related reports in such a way that readers can rapidly become acquainted with a large body of material without having to read it all. It will usually contain a brief statement of the problem or proposal covered in the major document(s), background information, concise analysis and main conclusions. It is intended as an aid to decision making by business managers.

a. ADTECH
b. AMAX
c. ACNielsen
d. Executive summary

16. _________ or _________ data refers to selected population characteristics as used in government, marketing or opinion research, or the _________ profiles used in such research. Note the distinction from the term 'demography' Commonly-used _________ include race, age, income, disabilities, mobility (in terms of travel time to work or number of vehicles available), educational attainment, home ownership, employment status, and even location.

a. Demographic
b. African Americans
c. Albert Einstein
d. AStore

17. An _________ is the manufacturing of a good or service within a category. Although _________ is a broad term for any kind of economic production, in economics and urban planning _________ is a synonym for the secondary sector, which is a type of economic activity involved in the manufacturing of raw materials into goods and products.

There are four key industrial economic sectors: the primary sector, largely raw material extraction industries such as mining and farming; the secondary sector, involving refining, construction, and manufacturing; the tertiary sector, which deals with services (such as law and medicine) and distribution of manufactured goods; and the quaternary sector, a relatively new type of knowledge _________ focusing on technological research, design and development such as computer programming, and biochemistry.

a. Industry
b. AMAX
c. ADTECH
d. ACNielsen

1. _________ is defined by the American _________ Association as the activity, set of institutions, and processes for creating, communicating, delivering, and exchanging offerings that have value for customers, clients, partners, and society at large. The term developed from the original meaning which referred literally to going to market, as in shopping, or going to a market to sell goods or services.

_________ practice tends to be seen as a creative industry, which includes advertising, distribution and selling.

a. Marketing myopia
b. Customer acquisition management
c. Product naming
d. Marketing

2. Consumer market research is a form of applied sociology that concentrates on understanding the behaviours, whims and preferences, of consumers in a market-based economy, and aims to understand the effects and comparative success of marketing campaigns. The field of consumer _________ as a statistical science was pioneered by Arthur Nielsen with the founding of the ACNielsen Company in 1923 .

Thus _________ is the systematic and objective identification, collection, analysis, and dissemination of information for the purpose of assisting management in decision making related to the identification and solution of problems and opportunities in marketing.

a. Focus group
b. Logit analysis
c. Marketing research process
d. Marketing research

3. A _________ attribute is one that exists in a range of magnitudes, and can therefore be measured. Measurements of any particular _________ property are expressed as a specific quantity, referred to as a unit, multiplied by a number. Examples of physical quantities are distance, mass, and time.
a. Dolly Dimples
b. Lifestyle city
c. Quantitative
d. BeyondROI

4. _________ refer to a collection of facts usually collected as the result of experience, observation or experiment or a set of premises. This may consist of numbers, words particularly as measurements or observations of a set of variables. _________ are often viewed as a lowest level of abstraction from which information and knowledge are derived.

a. Mean
b. Data
c. Sample size
d. Pearson product-moment correlation coefficient

5. A personal and cultural _________ is a relative ethic _________, an assumption upon which implementation can be extrapolated. A _________ system is a set of consistent _________s and measures that is soo not true. A principle _________ is a foundation upon which other _________s and measures of integrity are based.
a. Package-on-Package
b. Supreme Court of the United States
c. Value
d. Perceptual maps

6. _________ is a standard point of view or personal prejudice. especially when the tendency interferes with the ability to be impartial, unprejudiced, or objective. The term _________ed is used to describe an action, judgment, or other outcome influenced by a prejudged perspective.
a. Power III
b. Bias
c. 180SearchAssistant
d. 6-3-5 Brainwriting

7. _________ is a branch of philosophy which seeks to address questions about morality, such as how a moral outcome can be achieved in a specific situation (applied _________), how moral values should be determined (normative _________), what moral values people actually abide by (descriptive _________), what the fundamental semantic, ontological, and epistemic nature of _________ or morality is (meta-_________), and how moral capacity or moral agency develops and what its nature is (moral psychology.)

Socrates was one of the first Greek philosophers to encourage both scholars and the common citizen to turn their attention from the outside world to the condition of man. In this view, Knowledge having a bearing on human life was placed highest, all other knowledge being secondary.

a. ACNielsen
b. AMAX
c. ADTECH
d. Ethics

8. _________ is a process of gathering, modeling, and transforming data with the goal of highlighting useful information, suggesting conclusions, and supporting decision making. _________ has multiple facets and approaches, encompassing diverse techniques under a variety of names, in different business, science, and social science domains.

Data mining is a particular _________ technique that focuses on modeling and knowledge discovery for predictive rather than purely descriptive purposes.

a. Data analysis
b. 180SearchAssistant
c. Power III
d. 6-3-5 Brainwriting

9. In statistics, the _________ is a common measure of the correlation (linear dependence) between two variables X and Y. It is very widely used in the sciences as a measure of the strength of linear dependence between two variables, giving a value somewhere between +1 and -1 inclusive. It was first introduced by Francis Galton in the 1880s, and named after Karl Pearson.

In accordance with the usual convention, when calculated for an entire population, the Pearson product-moment correlation is typically designated by the analogous Greek letter, which in this case is ρ .

a. Median
b. Control chart
c. Standard deviation
d. Pearson product-moment correlation coefficient

10. In probability theory and statistics, _________ indicates the strength and direction of a linear relationship between two random variables. That is in contrast with the usage of the term in colloquial speech, denoting any relationship, not necessarily linear. In general statistical usage, _________ or co-relation refers to the departure of two random variables from independence.

a. Mean
b. Probability
c. Frequency distribution
d. Correlation

11. A _________ is a research instrument consisting of a series of questions and other prompts for the purpose of gathering information from respondents. Although they are often designed for statistical analysis of the responses, this is not always the case. The _________ was invented by Sir Francis Galton.

a. Mystery shopping
b. Questionnaire
c. Mystery shoppers
d. Market research

12. _________ is a telephone surveying technique in which the interviewer follows a script provided by a software application. The software is able to customize the flow of the questionnaire based on the answers provided, as well as information already known about the participant.

CATI may function in the following manner

- A computerized questionnaire is administered to respondents over the telephone.
- The interviewer sits in front of a computer screen
- Upon command, the computer dials the telephone number to be called.
- When contact is made, the interviewer reads the questions posed on the computer screen and records the respondent's answers directly into the computer.
- Interim and update reports can be compiled instantaneously, as the data are being collected.
- CATI software has built-in logic, which also enhances data accuracy.
- The program will personalize questions and control for logically incorrect answers, such as percentage answers that do not add up to 100 percent.
- The software has built-in branching logic, which will skip questions that are not applicable or will probe for more detail when warranted.

.

a. 180SearchAssistant
b. Computer-assisted telephone interviewing
c. 6-3-5 Brainwriting
d. Power III

13. _________ are used to collect quantitative information about items in a population. Surveys of human populations and institutions are common in political polling and government, health, social science and marketing research. A survey may focus on opinions or factual information depending on its purpose, and many surveys involve administering questions to individuals.
a. Convergent
b. Gross Margin Return on Inventory Investment
c. BeyondROI
d. Statistical surveys

14. _________ is a mathematical science pertaining to the collection, analysis, interpretation or explanation, and presentation of data. It also provides tools for prediction and forecasting based on data. It is applicable to a wide variety of academic disciplines, from the natural and social sciences to the humanities, government and business.

a. Null hypothesis
b. Median
c. Type I error
d. Statistics

15. _________ are used to describe the basic features of the data gathered from an experimental study in various ways. A _________ is distinguished from inductive statistics. They provide simple summaries about the sample and the measures.

a. Pearson product-moment correlation coefficient
b. Frequency distribution
c. P-Value
d. Descriptive statistics

16. In statistics, a _________ is a tabulation of the values that one or more variables take in a sample.

Univariate _________s are often presented as lists, ordered by quantity, showing the number of times each value appears. For example, if 100 people rate a five-point Likert scale assessing their agreement with a statement on a scale on which 1 denotes strong agreement and 5 strong disagreement, the _________ of their responses might look like:

This simple tabulation has two drawbacks.

a. Survey research
b. Confidence interval
c. Frequency distribution
d. Statistics

17. _________ is one of the four elements of marketing mix. An organization or set of organizations (go-betweens) involved in the process of making a product or service available for use or consumption by a consumer or business user.

The other three parts of the marketing mix are product, pricing, and promotion.

a. Better Living Through Chemistry
b. Comparison-Shopping agent
c. Japan Advertising Photographers' Association
d. Distribution

18. In statistics, analysis of variance (_________) is a collection of statistical models, and their associated procedures, in which the observed variance is partitioned into components due to different explanatory variables. In its simplest form _________ gives a statistical test of whether the means of several groups are all equal, and therefore generalizes Student's two-sample t-test to more than two groups.

There are three conceptual classes of such models:

1. Fixed-effects models assumes that the data came from normal populations which may differ only in their means. (Model 1)
2. Random effects models assume that the data describe a hierarchy of different populations whose differences are constrained by the hierarchy. (Model 2)
3. Mixed-effect models describe situations where both fixed and random effects are present. (Model 3)

In practice, there are several types of _________ depending on the number of treatments and the way they are applied to the subjects in the experiment:

- One-way _________ is used to test for differences among two or more independent groups. Typically, however, the one-way _________ is used to test for differences among at least three groups, since the two-group case can be covered by a T-test (Gossett, 1908.)

a. AMAX
b. ACNielsen
c. ANOVA
d. ADTECH

19. In statistics, _________ has two related meanings:

- the arithmetic _________
- the expected value of a random variable, which is also called the population _________.

It is sometimes stated that the '_________' _________s average. This is incorrect if '_________' is taken in the specific sense of 'arithmetic _________' as there are different types of averages: the _________, median, and mode. For instance, average house prices almost always use the median value for the average. These three types of averages are all measures of locations.

a. Confidence interval
b. Standard normal distribution
c. Mean
d. Heteroskedastic

20. In probability theory and statistics, a _________ is described as the number separating the higher half of a sample, a population from the lower half. The _________ of a finite list of numbers can be found by arranging all the observations from lowest value to highest value and picking the middle one. If there is an even number of observations, the _________ is not unique, so one often takes the mean of the two middle values.

a. Frequency distribution
b. Statistically significant
c. Linear regression
d. Median

21. In descriptive statistics, the _________ is the length of the smallest interval which contains all the data. It is calculated by subtracting the smallest observation (sample minimum) from the greatest (sample maximum) and provides an indication of statistical dispersion.

It is measured in the same units as the data.

a. Japan Advertising Photographers' Association
b. Just-In-Case
c. Personalization
d. Range

22. In statistics, _________ is a simple measure of the variability or dispersion of a data set. A low _________ indicates that the data points tend to be very close to the same value (the mean), while high _________ indicates that the data are 'spread out' over a large range of values.

For example, the average height for adult men in the United States is about 70 inches, with a _________ of around 3 inches.

a. Pearson product-moment correlation coefficient
b. Z-test
c. Statistically significant
d. Standard deviation

1. A _________ attribute is one that exists in a range of magnitudes, and can therefore be measured. Measurements of any particular _________ property are expressed as a specific quantity, referred to as a unit, multiplied by a number. Examples of physical quantities are distance, mass, and time.
 a. Dolly Dimples
 b. BeyondROI
 c. Quantitative
 d. Lifestyle city

2. _________ refer to a collection of facts usually collected as the result of experience, observation or experiment or a set of premises. This may consist of numbers, words particularly as measurements or observations of a set of variables. _________ are often viewed as a lowest level of abstraction from which information and knowledge are derived.
 a. Data
 b. Mean
 c. Sample size
 d. Pearson product-moment correlation coefficient

3. In statistics, analysis of variance (_________) is a collection of statistical models, and their associated procedures, in which the observed variance is partitioned into components due to different explanatory variables. In its simplest form _________ gives a statistical test of whether the means of several groups are all equal, and therefore generalizes Student's two-sample t-test to more than two groups.

There are three conceptual classes of such models:

1. Fixed-effects models assumes that the data came from normal populations which may differ only in their means. (Model 1)
2. Random effects models assume that the data describe a hierarchy of different populations whose differences are constrained by the hierarchy. (Model 2)
3. Mixed-effect models describe situations where both fixed and random effects are present. (Model 3)

In practice, there are several types of _________ depending on the number of treatments and the way they are applied to the subjects in the experiment:

- One-way _________ is used to test for differences among two or more independent groups. Typically, however, the one-way _________ is used to test for differences among at least three groups, since the two-group case can be covered by a T-test (Gossett, 1908.)

 a. AMAX
 b. ACNielsen
 c. ANOVA
 d. ADTECH

4. In statistics, _________ has two related meanings:

- the arithmetic _________
- the expected value of a random variable, which is also called the population _________.

It is sometimes stated that the '_________' _________s average. This is incorrect if '_________' is taken in the specific sense of 'arithmetic _________' as there are different types of averages: the _________, median, and mode. For instance, average house prices almost always use the median value for the average. These three types of averages are all measures of locations.

a. Confidence interval
b. Standard normal distribution
c. Mean
d. Heteroskedastic

5. _________ are used to collect quantitative information about items in a population. Surveys of human populations and institutions are common in political polling and government, health, social science and marketing research. A survey may focus on opinions or factual information depending on its purpose, and many surveys involve administering questions to individuals.
a. Statistical surveys
b. BeyondROI
c. Convergent
d. Gross Margin Return on Inventory Investment

6. _________ is a computer program used for statistical analysis.

_________ (originally, Statistical Package for the Social Sciences) was released in its first version in 1968 after being founded by Norman Nie and C. Hadlai Hull. Nie was then a political science postgraduate at Stanford University,and now Research Professor in the Department of Political Science at Stanford and Professor Emeritus of Political Science at the University of Chicago.

a. 6-3-5 Brainwriting
b. 180SearchAssistant
c. Power III
d. SPSS

7. A personal and cultural _________ is a relative ethic _________, an assumption upon which implementation can be extrapolated. A _________ system is a set of consistent _________s and measures that is soo not true. A principle _________ is a foundation upon which other _________s and measures of integrity are based.

a. Supreme Court of the United States
b. Package-on-Package
c. Perceptual maps
d. Value

8. In probability theory and statistics, a _________ is described as the number separating the higher half of a sample, a population from the lower half. The _________ of a finite list of numbers can be found by arranging all the observations from lowest value to highest value and picking the middle one. If there is an even number of observations, the _________ is not unique, so one often takes the mean of the two middle values.
a. Frequency distribution
b. Statistically significant
c. Linear regression
d. Median

9. In descriptive statistics, the _________ is the length of the smallest interval which contains all the data. It is calculated by subtracting the smallest observation (sample minimum) from the greatest (sample maximum) and provides an indication of statistical dispersion.

It is measured in the same units as the data.

a. Just-In-Case
b. Personalization
c. Range
d. Japan Advertising Photographers' Association

10. In statistics, _________ is a simple measure of the variability or dispersion of a data set. A low _________ indicates that the data points tend to be very close to the same value (the mean), while high _________ indicates that the data are 'spread out' over a large range of values.

For example, the average height for adult men in the United States is about 70 inches, with a _________ of around 3 inches.

a. Standard deviation
b. Statistically significant
c. Z-test
d. Pearson product-moment correlation coefficient

11. In statistics, _________ is a collection of statistical models, and their associated procedures, in which the observed variance is partitioned into components due to different explanatory variables. The initial techniques of the _________ were developed by the statistician and geneticist R. A. Fisher in the 1920s and 1930s, and is sometimes known as Fisher's ANOVA or Fisher's _________, due to the use of Fisher's F-distribution as part of the test of statistical significance.

There are three conceptual classes of such models:

1. Fixed-effects models assumes that the data came from normal populations which may differ only in their means. (Model 1)
2. Random effects models assume that the data describe a hierarchy of different populations whose differences are constrained by the hierarchy. (Model 2)
3. Mixed-effect models describe situations where both fixed and random effects are present. (Model 3)

In practice, there are several types of ANOVA depending on the number of treatments and the way they are applied to the subjects in the experiment:

- One-way ANOVA is used to test for differences among two or more independent groups. Typically, however, the One-way ANOVA is used to test for differences among at least three groups, since the two-group case can be covered by a T-test (Gossett, 1908.)

a. ACNielsen
b. Analysis of variance
c. Arithmetic mean
d. Interval estimation

12. In statistics, the _________ is a common measure of the correlation (linear dependence) between two variables X and Y. It is very widely used in the sciences as a measure of the strength of linear dependence between two variables, giving a value somewhere between +1 and -1 inclusive. It was first introduced by Francis Galton in the 1880s, and named after Karl Pearson.

In accordance with the usual convention, when calculated for an entire population, the Pearson product-moment correlation is typically designated by the analogous Greek letter, which in this case is ρ .

a. Control chart
b. Pearson product-moment correlation coefficient
c. Standard deviation
d. Median

13. In probability theory and statistics, _________ indicates the strength and direction of a linear relationship between two random variables. That is in contrast with the usage of the term in colloquial speech, denoting any relationship, not necessarily linear. In general statistical usage, _________ or co-relation refers to the departure of two random variables from independence.

a. Correlation
b. Frequency distribution
c. Mean
d. Probability

14. In probability theory and statistics, the _________ of a random variable, probability distribution, or sample is a measure of statistical dispersion, averaging the squared distance of its possible values from the expected value (mean.) Whereas the mean is a way to describe the location of a distribution, the _________ is a way to capture its scale or degree of being spread out. The unit of _________ is the square of the unit of the original variable.

a. Variance
b. Correlation
c. Standard deviation
d. Sample size

15. 'Speaking generally, properties are those physical quantities which directly describe the physical attributes of the system; _________s are those combinations of the properties which suffice to determine the response of the system. Properties can have all sorts of dimensions, depending upon the system being considered; _________s are dimensionless, or have the dimension of time or its reciprocal.'

The term can also be used in engineering contexts, however, as it is typically used in the physical sciences.

When the terms formal _________ and actual _________ are used, they generally correspond with the definitions used in computer science.

a. Parameter
b. Power III
c. 180SearchAssistant
d. 6-3-5 Brainwriting

16. _________ is a mathematical science pertaining to the collection, analysis, interpretation or explanation, and presentation of data. It also provides tools for prediction and forecasting based on data. It is applicable to a wide variety of academic disciplines, from the natural and social sciences to the humanities, government and business.

a. Null hypothesis
b. Type I error
c. Median
d. Statistics

17. The _________ and the null hypothesis are the two rival hypotheses whose likelihoods are compared by a statistical hypothesis test. Usually the _________ is the possibility that an observed effect is genuine and the null hypothesis is the rival possibility that it has resulted from chance.

The classical (or frequentist) approach is to calculate the probability that the observed effect (or one more extreme) will occur if the null hypothesis is true.

a. Interval estimation
b. Alternative hypothesis
c. Analysis of variance
d. ACNielsen

18. In statistics, a _________ is a tabulation of the values that one or more variables take in a sample.

Univariate _________s are often presented as lists, ordered by quantity, showing the number of times each value appears. For example, if 100 people rate a five-point Likert scale assessing their agreement with a statement on a scale on which 1 denotes strong agreement and 5 strong disagreement, the _________ of their responses might look like:

This simple tabulation has two drawbacks.

a. Confidence interval
b. Survey research
c. Frequency distribution
d. Statistics

19. _________ is one of the four elements of marketing mix. An organization or set of organizations (go-betweens) involved in the process of making a product or service available for use or consumption by a consumer or business user.

The other three parts of the marketing mix are product, pricing, and promotion.

a. Better Living Through Chemistry
b. Japan Advertising Photographers' Association
c. Comparison-Shopping agent
d. Distribution

20. _________ is a process of gathering, modeling, and transforming data with the goal of highlighting useful information, suggesting conclusions, and supporting decision making. _________ has multiple facets and approaches, encompassing diverse techniques under a variety of names, in different business, science, and social science domains.

Data mining is a particular _________ technique that focuses on modeling and knowledge discovery for predictive rather than purely descriptive purposes.

a. Data analysis
b. 180SearchAssistant
c. 6-3-5 Brainwriting
d. Power III

21. _________ or _________ data refers to selected population characteristics as used in government, marketing or opinion research, or the _________ profiles used in such research. Note the distinction from the term 'demography' Commonly-used _________ include race, age, income, disabilities, mobility (in terms of travel time to work or number of vehicles available), educational attainment, home ownership, employment status, and even location.
a. AStore
b. African Americans
c. Albert Einstein
d. Demographic

22. _________s are used in open sentences. For instance, in the formula x + 1 = 5, x is a _________ which represents an 'unknown' number. _________s are often represented by letters of the Roman alphabet, or those of other alphabets, such as Greek, and use other special symbols.
a. Book of business
b. Personalization
c. Variable
d. Quantitative

23. An example of a repeated measures _________ would be if one group were pre- and post-tested. (This example occurs in education quite frequently.) If a teacher wanted to examine the effect of a new set of textbooks on student achievement, (s)he could test the class at the beginning of the year (pretest) and at the end of the year (posttest.)

a. T-test
b. Null hypothesis
c. Moving average
d. Statistically significant

24. In statistical hypothesis testing, the _________ formally describes some aspect of the statistical behaviour of a set of data; this description is treated as valid unless the actual behaviour of the data contradicts this assumption. Thus, the _________ is contrasted against another hypothesis. Statistical hypothesis testing is used to make a decision about whether the data contradicts the _________: this is called significance testing.
a. Null hypothesis
b. Statistical hypothesis test
c. Standard score
d. Variance

25. In statistics, a result is called _________ if it is unlikely to have occurred by chance. 'A _________ difference' simply means there is statistical evidence that there is a difference; it does not mean the difference is necessarily large, important, or significant in the common meaning of the word.

The significance level of a test is a traditional frequentist statistical hypothesis testing concept.

a. Standard deviation
b. Randomization
c. Statistically significant
d. Frequency distribution

26. In statistics, a _________ is an interval estimate of a population parameter. Instead of estimating the parameter by a single value, an interval likely to include the parameter is given. Thus, _________s are used to indicate the reliability of an estimate.
a. Sample mean
b. T-test
c. Linear regression
d. Confidence interval

27. _________ is a form of communication that typically attempts to persuade potential customers to purchase or to consume more of a particular brand of product or service. 'While now central to the contemporary global economy and the reproduction of global production networks, it is only quite recently that _________ has been more than a marginal influence on patterns of sales and production. The formation of modern _________ was intimately bound up with the emergence of new forms of monopoly capitalism around the end of the 19th and beginning of the 20th century as one element in corporate strategies to create, organize and where possible control markets, especially for mass produced consumer goods.

a. ADTECH
b. ACNielsen
c. AMAX
d. Advertising

28. _________ is a graphics technique used by asset marketers that attempts to visually display the perceptions of customers or potential customers. Typically the position of a product, product line, brand, or company is displayed relative to their competition.

Perceptual maps can have any number of dimensions but the most common is two dimensions.

a. Perceptual mapping
b. Market environment
c. Kano model
d. Customer franchise

29. _________ is defined by the American _________ Association as the activity, set of institutions, and processes for creating, communicating, delivering, and exchanging offerings that have value for customers, clients, partners, and society at large. The term developed from the original meaning which referred literally to going to market, as in shopping, or going to a market to sell goods or services.

_________ practice tends to be seen as a creative industry, which includes advertising, distribution and selling.

a. Marketing myopia
b. Customer acquisition management
c. Product naming
d. Marketing

30. _________ in organizations and public policy is both the organizational process of creating and maintaining a plan; and the psychological process of thinking about the activities required to create a desired goal on some scale. As such, it is a fundamental property of intelligent behavior. This thought process is essential to the creation and refinement of a plan, or integration of it with other plans, that is, it combines forecasting of developments with the preparation of scenarios of how to react to them.

a. 180SearchAssistant
b. 6-3-5 Brainwriting
c. Power III
d. Planning

31. In marketing, _________ has come to mean the process by which marketers try to create an image or identity in the minds of their target market for its product, brand, or organization. It is the 'relative competitive comparison' their product occupies in a given market as perceived by the target market.

Re-_________ involves changing the identity of a product, relative to the identity of competing products, in the collective minds of the target market.

a. Containerization
b. Positioning
c. GE matrix
d. Moratorium

1. A _________ is a collection of symbols, experiences and associations connected with a product, a service, a person or any other artifact or entity.

_________s have become increasingly important components of culture and the economy, now being described as 'cultural accessories and personal philosophies'.

Some people distinguish the psychological aspect of a _________ from the experiential aspect.

a. Store brand
b. Brandable software
c. Brand equity
d. Brand

2. Procter is a surname, and may also refer to:

- Bryan Waller Procter (pseud. Barry Cornwall), English poet
- Goodwin Procter, American law firm
- _________, consumer products multinational

.

a. Convergent
b. Procter ' Gamble
c. Black PRies
d. Flyer

3. _________ consists of the processes a company uses to track and organize its contacts with its current and prospective customers. _________ software is used to support these processes; information about customers and customer interactions can be entered, stored and accessed by employees in different company departments. Typical _________ goals are to improve services provided to customers, and to use customer contact information for targeted marketing.
a. Product bundling
b. Demand generation
c. Commercialization
d. Customer relationship management

4. _________ refer to a collection of facts usually collected as the result of experience, observation or experiment or a set of premises. This may consist of numbers, words particularly as measurements or observations of a set of variables. _________ are often viewed as a lowest level of abstraction from which information and knowledge are derived.

a. Mean
b. Sample size
c. Pearson product-moment correlation coefficient
d. Data

5. _________ is the process of extracting hidden patterns from data. As more data is gathered, with the amount of data doubling every three years, _________ is becoming an increasingly important tool to transform this data into information. It is commonly used in a wide range of profiling practices, such as marketing, surveillance, fraud detection and scientific discovery.
a. Structure mining
b. 180SearchAssistant
c. Power III
d. Data mining

6. Customer _________ consists of the processes a company uses to track and organize its contacts with its current and prospective customers. CRelationship management software is used to support these processes; information about customers and customer interactions can be entered, stored and accessed by employees in different company departments. Typical CRelationship management goals are to improve services provided to customers, and to use customer contact information for targeted marketing.
a. Relationship management
b. Product bundling
c. Marketing
d. Green marketing

7. In probability theory and statistics, _________ indicates the strength and direction of a linear relationship between two random variables. That is in contrast with the usage of the term in colloquial speech, denoting any relationship, not necessarily linear. In general statistical usage, _________ or co-relation refers to the departure of two random variables from independence.
a. Correlation
b. Mean
c. Frequency distribution
d. Probability

8. In statistics, the _________ is a common measure of the correlation (linear dependence) between two variables X and Y. It is very widely used in the sciences as a measure of the strength of linear dependence between two variables, giving a value somewhere between +1 and -1 inclusive. It was first introduced by Francis Galton in the 1880s, and named after Karl Pearson.

In accordance with the usual convention, when calculated for an entire population, the Pearson product-moment correlation is typically designated by the analogous Greek letter, which in this case is ρ .

a. Pearson product-moment correlation coefficient
b. Control chart
c. Standard deviation
d. Median

9. In statistics, a result is called _________ if it is unlikely to have occurred by chance. 'A _________ difference' simply means there is statistical evidence that there is a difference; it does not mean the difference is necessarily large, important, or significant in the common meaning of the word.

The significance level of a test is a traditional frequentist statistical hypothesis testing concept.

a. Frequency distribution
b. Standard deviation
c. Statistically significant
d. Randomization

10. In statistics, the _________, R^2 is used in the context of statistical models whose main purpose is the prediction of future outcomes on the basis of other related information. It is the proportion of variability in a data set that is accounted for by the statistical model. It provides a measure of how well future outcomes are likely to be predicted by the model.
a. Multicollinearity
b. Regression analysis
c. Variance inflation factor
d. Coefficient of determination

11. In statistics, _________ is a collective name for techniques for the modeling and analysis of numerical data consisting of values of a dependent variable and of one or more independent variables The dependent variable in the regression equation is modeled as a function of the independent variables, corresponding parameters, and an error term. The error term is treated as a random variable.
a. Multicollinearity
b. Stepwise regression
c. Variance inflation factor
d. Regression analysis

12. In statistical hypothesis testing, the _________ formally describes some aspect of the statistical behaviour of a set of data; this description is treated as valid unless the actual behaviour of the data contradicts this assumption. Thus, the _________ is contrasted against another hypothesis. Statistical hypothesis testing is used to make a decision about whether the data contradicts the _________: this is called significance testing.

a. Standard score
b. Variance
c. Null hypothesis
d. Statistical hypothesis test

13. The _________ of a test is a traditional frequentist statistical hypothesis testing concept. In simple cases, it is defined as the probability of making a decision to reject the null hypothesis when the null hypothesis is actually true (a decision known as a Type I error, or 'false positive determination'.) The decision is often made using the p-value: if the p-value is less than the _________, then the null hypothesis is rejected.

a. Significance level
b. Statistical hypothesis test
c. Type I error
d. Standard deviation

14. _________ is a computer program used for statistical analysis.

_________ (originally, Statistical Package for the Social Sciences) was released in its first version in 1968 after being founded by Norman Nie and C. Hadlai Hull. Nie was then a political science postgraduate at Stanford University,and now Research Professor in the Department of Political Science at Stanford and Professor Emeritus of Political Science at the University of Chicago.

a. Power III
b. 180SearchAssistant
c. 6-3-5 Brainwriting
d. SPSS

15. _________ is one of the four elements of marketing mix. An organization or set of organizations (go-betweens) involved in the process of making a product or service available for use or consumption by a consumer or business user.

The other three parts of the marketing mix are product, pricing, and promotion.

a. Japan Advertising Photographers' Association
b. Comparison-Shopping agent
c. Better Living Through Chemistry
d. Distribution

16. In probability theory and statistics, a _________ is described as the number separating the higher half of a sample, a population from the lower half. The _________ of a finite list of numbers can be found by arranging all the observations from lowest value to highest value and picking the middle one. If there is an even number of observations, the _________ is not unique, so one often takes the mean of the two middle values.
a. Linear regression
b. Statistically significant
c. Frequency distribution
d. Median

17. In statistics, analysis of variance (_________) is a collection of statistical models, and their associated procedures, in which the observed variance is partitioned into components due to different explanatory variables. In its simplest form _________ gives a statistical test of whether the means of several groups are all equal, and therefore generalizes Student's two-sample t-test to more than two groups.

There are three conceptual classes of such models:

1. Fixed-effects models assumes that the data came from normal populations which may differ only in their means. (Model 1)
2. Random effects models assume that the data describe a hierarchy of different populations whose differences are constrained by the hierarchy. (Model 2)
3. Mixed-effect models describe situations where both fixed and random effects are present. (Model 3)

In practice, there are several types of _________ depending on the number of treatments and the way they are applied to the subjects in the experiment:

- One-way _________ is used to test for differences among two or more independent groups. Typically, however, the one-way _________ is used to test for differences among at least three groups, since the two-group case can be covered by a T-test (Gossett, 1908.)

a. ACNielsen
b. ADTECH
c. AMAX
d. ANOVA

18. In probability theory and statistics, the _________ of a random variable, probability distribution, or sample is a measure of statistical dispersion, averaging the squared distance of its possible values from the expected value (mean.) Whereas the mean is a way to describe the location of a distribution, the _________ is a way to capture its scale or degree of being spread out. The unit of _________ is the square of the unit of the original variable.

a. Variance
b. Correlation
c. Standard deviation
d. Sample size

19. In statistics, _________ is used for two things;

- to construct a simple formula that will predict what value will occur for a quantity of interest when other related variables take given values.
- to allow a test to be made of whether a given variable does have an effect on a quantity of interest in situations where there may be many related variables.

In both cases, several sets of outcomes are available for the quantity of interest together with the related variables.

_________ is a form of regression analysis in which the relationship between one or more independent variables and another variable, called the dependent variable, is modelled by a least squares function, called a _________ equation. This function is a linear combination of one or more model parameters, called regression coefficients. A _________ equation with one independent variable represents a straight line when the predicted value (i.e. the dependant variable from the regression equation) is plotted against the independent variable: this is called a simple _________.

a. Descriptive statistics
b. Sample size
c. Heteroskedastic
d. Linear regression

20. _________ is a statistical phenomenon in which two or more predictor variables in a multiple regression model are highly correlated. In this situation the coefficient estimates may change erratically in response to small changes in the model or the data. _________ does not reduce the predictive power or reliability of the model as a whole; it only affects calculations regarding individual predictors.

a. Variance inflation factor
b. Regression analysis
c. Multicollinearity
d. Stepwise regression

21. _________, a business term, is a measure of how products and services supplied by a company meet or surpass customer expectation. It is seen as a key performance indicator within business and is part of the four perspectives of a Balanced Scorecard.

In a competitive marketplace where businesses compete for customers, _________ is seen as a key differentiator and increasingly has become a key element of business strategy.

a. Supplier diversity
b. Psychological pricing
c. Customer base
d. Customer satisfaction

1. A _________ attribute is one that exists in a range of magnitudes, and can therefore be measured. Measurements of any particular _________ property are expressed as a specific quantity, referred to as a unit, multiplied by a number. Examples of physical quantities are distance, mass, and time.

a. Dolly Dimples
b. Quantitative
c. BeyondROI
d. Lifestyle city

2. _________ is defined by the American _________ Association as the activity, set of institutions, and processes for creating, communicating, delivering, and exchanging offerings that have value for customers, clients, partners, and society at large. The term developed from the original meaning which referred literally to going to market, as in shopping, or going to a market to sell goods or services.

_________ practice tends to be seen as a creative industry, which includes advertising, distribution and selling.

a. Marketing
b. Marketing myopia
c. Customer acquisition management
d. Product naming

3. Consumer market research is a form of applied sociology that concentrates on understanding the behaviours, whims and preferences, of consumers in a market-based economy, and aims to understand the effects and comparative success of marketing campaigns. The field of consumer _________ as a statistical science was pioneered by Arthur Nielsen with the founding of the ACNielsen Company in 1923 .

Thus _________ is the systematic and objective identification, collection, analysis, and dissemination of information for the purpose of assisting management in decision making related to the identification and solution of problems and opportunities in marketing.

a. Focus group
b. Logit analysis
c. Marketing research process
d. Marketing research

4. _________ refer to a collection of facts usually collected as the result of experience, observation or experiment or a set of premises. This may consist of numbers, words particularly as measurements or observations of a set of variables. _________ are often viewed as a lowest level of abstraction from which information and knowledge are derived.

a. Sample size
b. Pearson product-moment correlation coefficient
c. Mean
d. Data

5. _________ is a process of gathering, modeling, and transforming data with the goal of highlighting useful information, suggesting conclusions, and supporting decision making. _________ has multiple facets and approaches, encompassing diverse techniques under a variety of names, in different business, science, and social science domains.

Data mining is a particular _________ technique that focuses on modeling and knowledge discovery for predictive rather than purely descriptive purposes.

a. 180SearchAssistant
b. Data analysis
c. 6-3-5 Brainwriting
d. Power III

6. _________ is a field of inquiry that crosscuts disciplines and subject matters . _________ers aim to gather an in-depth understanding of human behavior and the reasons that govern such behavior. The discipline investigates the why and how of decision making, not just what, where, when.
a. Power III
b. 180SearchAssistant
c. 6-3-5 Brainwriting
d. Qualitative research

7. A personal and cultural _________ is a relative ethic _________, an assumption upon which implementation can be extrapolated. A _________ system is a set of consistent _________s and measures that is soo not true. A principle _________ is a foundation upon which other _________s and measures of integrity are based.
a. Package-on-Package
b. Perceptual maps
c. Supreme Court of the United States
d. Value

8. _________ is a term used in business for a short document that summarises a longer report, proposal or group of related reports in such a way that readers can rapidly become acquainted with a large body of material without having to read it all. It will usually contain a brief statement of the problem or proposal covered in the major document(s), background information, concise analysis and main conclusions. It is intended as an aid to decision making by business managers.

a. ACNielsen
b. AMAX
c. ADTECH
d. Executive summary

9. A _________ is a research instrument consisting of a series of questions and other prompts for the purpose of gathering information from respondents. Although they are often designed for statistical analysis of the responses, this is not always the case. The _________ was invented by Sir Francis Galton.
a. Market research
b. Mystery shoppers
c. Mystery shopping
d. Questionnaire

10. In statistics, analysis of variance (_________) is a collection of statistical models, and their associated procedures, in which the observed variance is partitioned into components due to different explanatory variables. In its simplest form _________ gives a statistical test of whether the means of several groups are all equal, and therefore generalizes Student's two-sample t-test to more than two groups.

There are three conceptual classes of such models:

1. Fixed-effects models assumes that the data came from normal populations which may differ only in their means. (Model 1)
2. Random effects models assume that the data describe a hierarchy of different populations whose differences are constrained by the hierarchy. (Model 2)
3. Mixed-effect models describe situations where both fixed and random effects are present. (Model 3)

In practice, there are several types of _________ depending on the number of treatments and the way they are applied to the subjects in the experiment:

- One-way _________ is used to test for differences among two or more independent groups. Typically, however, the one-way _________ is used to test for differences among at least three groups, since the two-group case can be covered by a T-test (Gossett, 1908.)

a. AMAX
b. ACNielsen
c. ADTECH
d. ANOVA

11. _________ is a computer program used for statistical analysis.

_________ (originally, Statistical Package for the Social Sciences) was released in its first version in 1968 after being founded by Norman Nie and C. Hadlai Hull. Nie was then a political science postgraduate at Stanford University,and now Research Professor in the Department of Political Science at Stanford and Professor Emeritus of Political Science at the University of Chicago.

a. 180SearchAssistant
b. 6-3-5 Brainwriting
c. Power III
d. SPSS

12. In statistics, the _________ is a common measure of the correlation (linear dependence) between two variables X and Y. It is very widely used in the sciences as a measure of the strength of linear dependence between two variables, giving a value somewhere between +1 and -1 inclusive. It was first introduced by Francis Galton in the 1880s, and named after Karl Pearson.

In accordance with the usual convention, when calculated for an entire population, the Pearson product-moment correlation is typically designated by the analogous Greek letter, which in this case is ρ .

a. Standard deviation
b. Control chart
c. Median
d. Pearson product-moment correlation coefficient

13. In probability theory and statistics, _________ indicates the strength and direction of a linear relationship between two random variables. That is in contrast with the usage of the term in colloquial speech, denoting any relationship, not necessarily linear. In general statistical usage, _________ or co-relation refers to the departure of two random variables from independence.

a. Probability
b. Mean
c. Correlation
d. Frequency distribution

14. In statistics, _________ has two related meanings:

- the arithmetic _________
- the expected value of a random variable, which is also called the population _________.

It is sometimes stated that the '_________' _________s average. This is incorrect if '_________' is taken in the specific sense of 'arithmetic _________' as there are different types of averages: the _________, median, and mode. For instance, average house prices almost always use the median value for the average. These three types of averages are all measures of locations.

a. Standard normal distribution
b. Mean
c. Confidence interval
d. Heteroskedastic

15. _________s are used in open sentences. For instance, in the formula x + 1 = 5, x is a _________ which represents an 'unknown' number. _________s are often represented by letters of the Roman alphabet, or those of other alphabets, such as Greek, and use other special symbols.

a. Book of business
b. Quantitative
c. Personalization
d. Variable

16. In statistics, _________ is a collection of statistical models, and their associated procedures, in which the observed variance is partitioned into components due to different explanatory variables. The initial techniques of the _________ were developed by the statistician and geneticist R. A. Fisher in the 1920s and 1930s, and is sometimes known as Fisher's ANOVA or Fisher's _________, due to the use of Fisher's F-distribution as part of the test of statistical significance.

There are three conceptual classes of such models:

1. Fixed-effects models assumes that the data came from normal populations which may differ only in their means. (Model 1)
2. Random effects models assume that the data describe a hierarchy of different populations whose differences are constrained by the hierarchy. (Model 2)
3. Mixed-effect models describe situations where both fixed and random effects are present. (Model 3)

In practice, there are several types of ANOVA depending on the number of treatments and the way they are applied to the subjects in the experiment:

- One-way ANOVA is used to test for differences among two or more independent groups. Typically, however, the One-way ANOVA is used to test for differences among at least three groups, since the two-group case can be covered by a T-test (Gossett, 1908.)

a. ACNielsen
b. Interval estimation
c. Analysis of variance
d. Arithmetic mean

17. In statistics, _________ is a simple measure of the variability or dispersion of a data set. A low _________ indicates that the data points tend to be very close to the same value (the mean), while high _________ indicates that the data are 'spread out' over a large range of values.

For example, the average height for adult men in the United States is about 70 inches, with a _________ of around 3 inches.

a. Statistically significant
b. Pearson product-moment correlation coefficient
c. Z-test
d. Standard deviation

18. An example of a repeated measures _________ would be if one group were pre- and post-tested. (This example occurs in education quite frequently.) If a teacher wanted to examine the effect of a new set of textbooks on student achievement, (s)he could test the class at the beginning of the year (pretest) and at the end of the year (posttest.)

a. Statistically significant
b. Null hypothesis
c. T-test
d. Moving average

19. In probability theory and statistics, the _________ of a random variable, probability distribution, or sample is a measure of statistical dispersion, averaging the squared distance of its possible values from the expected value (mean.) Whereas the mean is a way to describe the location of a distribution, the _________ is a way to capture its scale or degree of being spread out. The unit of _________ is the square of the unit of the original variable.

a. Standard deviation
b. Correlation
c. Sample size
d. Variance

20. In statistics, _________ is a collective name for techniques for the modeling and analysis of numerical data consisting of values of a dependent variable and of one or more independent variables The dependent variable in the regression equation is modeled as a function of the independent variables, corresponding parameters, and an error term. The error term is treated as a random variable.

a. Regression analysis
b. Stepwise regression
c. Variance inflation factor
d. Multicollinearity

Chapter 1

1. c	2. a	3. d	4. d	5. a	6. c	7. b	8. d	9. b	10. a
11. b	12. c	13. a	14. d	15. d	16. d	17. d	18. d	19. a	20. d
21. d	22. d	23. d	24. b	25. c	26. d	27. b	28. b	29. d	30. c
31. d	32. b	33. a	34. d	35. a	36. d	37. c	38. a	39. a	40. d
41. c									

Chapter 2

1. a	2. d	3. d	4. a	5. d	6. d	7. c	8. d	9. a	10. d
11. c	12. a	13. d	14. d	15. b	16. c	17. d	18. c	19. b	20. c
21. b	22. d	23. c	24. d	25. d	26. d	27. c	28. d		

Chapter 3

1. a	2. d	3. c	4. d	5. d	6. d	7. b	8. d	9. a	10. a
11. d	12. b	13. d	14. a	15. d	16. d	17. d	18. b		

Chapter 4

1. a	2. d	3. d	4. c	5. b	6. b	7. a	8. a	9. c	10. d
11. d	12. a	13. a	14. d	15. c	16. d	17. b	18. d	19. a	20. c
21. c	22. d	23. a	24. d	25. d	26. b	27. c	28. b	29. b	30. a
31. d	32. d	33. d	34. a	35. c	36. c				

Chapter 5

1. d	2. d	3. b	4. d	5. d	6. d	7. a	8. b	9. c	10. d
11. b	12. d	13. a	14. d	15. c	16. b	17. d	18. c	19. c	20. c
21. b	22. a	23. d	24. c	25. d	26. b	27. c	28. b	29. d	30. b
31. d									

Chapter 6

1. d	2. d	3. a	4. b	5. c	6. d	7. d	8. d	9. d	10. d
11. d	12. b	13. b	14. d	15. d	16. c	17. b	18. d	19. d	20. c
21. d	22. a	23. c	24. d	25. b					

Chapter 7

1. d	2. d	3. a	4. d	5. a	6. c	7. a	8. d	9. a	10. d
11. d	12. c	13. b	14. d	15. c	16. c	17. a	18. c	19. a	20. d
21. b	22. d	23. d	24. d	25. b	26. b	27. a			

Chapter 8

1. d	2. a	3. d	4. d	5. d	6. d	7. c	8. b	9. d	10. c
11. d	12. b	13. d	14. d	15. a	16. d	17. b	18. d	19. d	20. c
21. d	22. d	23. b	24. d						

Chapter 9

1. c	2. d	3. b	4. b	5. d	6. b	7. d	8. d	9. d	10. a
11. b									

Chapter 10

1. a	2. d	3. c	4. c	5. d	6. d	7. b	8. d	9. c	10. c
11. c	12. c	13. d	14. b	15. d	16. a	17. a			

Chapter 11

1. d	2. d	3. c	4. b	5. c	6. b	7. d	8. a	9. d	10. d
11. b	12. b	13. d	14. d	15. d	16. c	17. d	18. c	19. c	20. d
21. d	22. d								

Chapter 12

1. c	2. a	3. c	4. c	5. a	6. d	7. d	8. d	9. c	10. a
11. b	12. b	13. a	14. a	15. a	16. d	17. b	18. c	19. d	20. a
21. d	22. c	23. a	24. a	25. c	26. d	27. d	28. a	29. d	30. d
31. b									

Chapter 13

1. d	2. b	3. d	4. d	5. d	6. a	7. a	8. a	9. c	10. d
11. d	12. c	13. a	14. d	15. d	16. d	17. d	18. a	19. d	20. c
21. d									

Chapter 14

1. b	2. a	3. d	4. d	5. b	6. d	7. d	8. d	9. d	10. d
11. d	12. d	13. c	14. b	15. d	16. c	17. d	18. c	19. d	20. a

www.ingramcontent.com/pod-product-compliance
Lightning Source LLC
Chambersburg PA
CBHW082050230426
43670CB00016B/2841
9781428872363